Wisdom of the Internet

Wisdom of the Internet

Inspirational quotes, Good-to-knows
and Shitposts

a Giant Blur Book

Beneath the sky, in mystic daze,
Amidst the trees the owlet plays.
Underneath it, in thick haze,
Zombies dance with tranquil grace.

Introduction

What started out as the typical memes-to-mantras folder on a phone became quite a big collection of posts and quotes over the years. I would browse through this collection whenever I had no Internet connection or needed some inspiration to get me going again.
A couple of years back when I lost my job, I fell into quite the hole and started writing up these quotes in a text file as a form of therapy. The text file turned into the book you are reading right now. I hope it will serve you, as it did me, as a companion, a beacon of light during dark times, or at least as something to waste some time with when the Internet is down.

The quotes are random and follow no particular logic. Embrace the chaos and may you find inspiration, motivation, fun, and a bit of wisdom in the following pages.

Thank you, (people of the) internet,
for dispensing your knowledge.

Disclaimer

The author and the publisher claim no responsibility for actions taken or not taken based on the content of this book.
This book does not constitute financial, legal, or any other form of professional advice. Readers seeking specific guidance should consult with qualified professionals relevant to their individual circumstances.

These quotes are presented for the purpose of inspiration, reflection, and discussion. No claim is made regarding the original authorship or copyright status of the quotes included. If you are curious about the original sources or authors of the quotes, be encouraged to look them up online.

Should this book offend you in any way, it is strongly suggested that you buy as many copies as possible and post a video on social media of you burning them all.

People who know a lot of quotes can't be
bad people.

We were made to encourage each other.

Only boring people are bored.

From error to error, one compiles the entire code.

You must want to spend the rest of your life with yourself first.

Good people do not need laws to tell them to act responsibly, while bad people will find a way around the laws.

We are drowning in information while starving for wisdom.

The shortcut you are looking for is called discipline.

Make your bed in the morning. It's a very simple task, and it will give you a sense of accomplishment right at the start of your day.

Treat your passwords like your underwear. Change them regularly.

Be your authentic self. Unless you want people to like you.

Nobody is really selfless. Everybody wants something.

When you're in a relationship with someone, and you've never had the opportunity to meet their friends or family, you should be concerned.

The obedient always think of themselves as virtuous rather than cowardly.

Have a shower towel and a towel for your face.

Floss. Walk 30 minutes a day, five days a week, even if it's just to the shop and back. Drink plenty of water. Have a firm handshake.

Have extra toothpaste and deodorant at home. And toilet paper.

Use the 75/15/10 rule for all the money that comes to you:
75% for needs and wants, 15% for buying assets, and 10% goes to high-yield savings account as a retirement fund. Start early. Follow strictly.

Being intimacy deprived is a real thing.

Once you stop caring, it's a wrap.

To live is the rarest thing in the world. Most people just exist.

Comfort zone. Learning zone. Growth zone.

Tolerance becomes a crime when applied to evil.

Think with your head, not with your pride.

Your smartphone is a tracking device that happens to make phone calls.

Distraction is the enemy of vision.

Holding onto anger is like drinking poison and expecting the other person to die.

Eat your veggies and fruits. Do not over-consume sugar, salt, and oil. Try to sleep 8 hours a day. Avoid tobacco and alcohol. Don't rush if you don't have to. Pay your debt.

Never buy a new car that just hit the market. Buy something that's at least 2 years old.

Studies have shown that intelligent people swear more than stupid motherfuckers.

The most important person in life is you. Life is about you, and you should enjoy it. Treat other people well, but don't forget they are just extras in your life. People come and go, so focus on what makes you happy.

Holding on to anger and resentment will leave you more alone than you can imagine. Let go.

If you see someone crying, ask if it's because of their haircut.

The number of people older than you never increases.

Be a minimalistic person; it saves a lot of money and helps you discover what you really want. And you will realize how few things you actually need.

Laxatives are the best cough medicine. Take a few pills, and you'll be very afraid to cough.

Nobody is ever too busy; it is just a matter of priorities.

97% of scientists agree with whoever is funding them.

Be more involved in life and less attached to it.

What's meant for you will always feel natural, calm and clear, not forced, chaotic, and confusing.

Switching to zero-drop shoes can be a life-changing decision.

When you find that people failed you, turn to shelter pets. People have failed them too; you could heal together.

Go outside. Go into the forest and search for portals to other dimensions.

Do it or don't do it. Time will pass anyway.

Work like you don't need the money. Dance like no one is watching. And love like you've never been hurt.

The occurrence of kangaroo-related roadkills in Australia is thought to be linked to driving on the left side of the road, unlike countries with right-side traffic where kangaroo roadkills are not reported.

There are no honest politicians. Most of them are just business people looking out for themselves.

Stop accepting things you are not okay with.

Potential doesn't get you anywhere. Doing the work does.

The beauty you see in anything is a reflection of the beauty in you.

Back up your data. Regularly. Do it now.

We trade our days for things.

If you are hungry but you are too tired to cook, try 30 to 40 olives. It's an easy snack, and you can eat them directly out of the jar with your fingers. And you will certainly not regret eating 30 to 40 olives.

Repressing emotions is not a sign of strength.

Don't walk away to teach people a lesson. Walk away because you learned yours.

Don't stop until you are proud. Then keep going.

Don't ask questions if you don't need to know the answer. You don't need to have an opinion about everything.

Emotions aren't facts. Reflect first.

You can't change the people around you, but you can change the people around you.

In nature, poisonous creatures will develop bright colors to warn others of their toxicity. Humans often do the same with the color of their hair.

If your parents gave you a normal upbringing, listen to their life advice.

It's better to be single and content than unhappy with somebody.

If you own a dog, don't be angry if your dog wants to spend time with you. You are their entire life, and they only live so long. Take walks with them as often as possible and allow them to sniff intensely whatever they want. They need the mental and physical stimulation.

Don't let loneliness make you reconnect with toxic people. You shouldn't drink poison just because you are thirsty.

The self is a problem that thought cannot resolve.

Go to the gym. Alone, or with friends if you can. Nobody ever complained how fucked their life is while focusing on a set.

There is no key to success, but the key to failure is trying to please everybody.

Dream big and take risks. If you succeed, you'll be happy. If you fail, you'll be smarter.

When searching for a house to purchase, arrive at the location approximately an hour before meeting with the realtor. Take the opportunity to introduce yourself to the neighbors. It's possible that you may find you don't like them, and striking up a conversation with them might yield valuable insights that the realtor may not provide. Neighbors often have a wealth of information to share.

Less egos, more amigos.

A candle's flame smells like burnt nose hair.

Find someone who ruins your lipstick, not your mascara.

People are so keen to put the details of their private life in public, they seem to forget that invisibility is a superpower.

You're your own worst critic. Don't be so hard on yourself.

You can make cucumbers last longer if you wrap them in a paper towel and put them in a plastic bag. Close the bag loosely. The cucumbers will stay fresh for up to nine days.

Worrying is a waste of time. If there is a solution to your problem, you don't have to worry. If there is no solution, worrying does not solve it either.

Obsessively hating people that you wouldn't even know about if you didn't have internet or a TV is the biggest waste of time and energy there is.

Everything will kill you, so choose something fun.

Nothing beats fish soup as a work lunch. Heat it up in a microwave if possible.

Don't worry about getting old; worry about thinking old.

Sometimes you miss the memory, not the person.

If you win a decent amount of money in gambling, stop or you will lose everything. The house always wins in the long run.

Be open-minded and willing to alter your belief system if necessary.

Don't forget your towel when hitchhiking.

The greatest inspiration is the deadline.

Play a live album during sex; that way you get an applause every three minutes.

The signature and the dick; be careful where you put those two things.

Stop wondering why you are not fitting into a toxic society.

Visit the woods. Often.

When traveling, stick a dryer sheet into your suitcase to keep your clothes fresh.

Get a taxi on your first date with someone. If they get in and scoot over so you can get in, they pass. If they close the door and make you walk around, stay vigilant.

Age should never be a barrier to pursuing your dreams. Growing older doesn't mean you can't strive to be the happiest and truest version of yourself.

Throughout the past five millennia, humans worshiped over 5000 different gods. Either all of them are real, which seems improbable; one is real, still highly unlikely; or they are all human constructs, created to manipulate and dominate.

Happiness is the best makeup.

Dogs are God's way of apologizing for your relatives.

Temporary people can teach us permanent lessons.

Be private. Not everyone wants what's best for you.

Unplug and go outside.

They got us fighting a culture war to stop us from fighting a class war.

Whether with a friend, a partner, or a family, the number one thing you need is communication.

If you want your Android phone to feel faster, activate developer mode. Go into the settings. Search for the build number and tap it multiple times until "I'm a developer" appears on the screen. Open the newly added "Developer Settings" and set animations to off.

We will always be haunted by the idea that we are wasting our life.

You don't always have to put foil over your food in the oven. You can put a baking sheet on the shelf above instead. Save foil.

Do all things with love.

The war will end, and the leaders will shake hands. You will not know who sold out the homeland. But you will know who paid the price.

A perfect marriage is just two imperfect people who refuse to give up on each other.

On a first date, the primary goal isn't to leave a strong impression but rather to ensure that the other person enjoys themselves. Genuine connections are forged through the emotions and experiences shared during the time spent together, not through showcasing your accomplishments.

Throughout your life, you'll encounter moments when your own mind presents you with compelling yet ultimately false ideas. It's easy to fall into the trap of believing them because, after all, it's your own mind, something you've inherently trusted for years. The mind can be mistaken. Know that your inner thoughts aren't infallible.

If you announce your goals too early, you are less likely to achieve them.

Always bring your own condoms.

Civilized men are more discourteous than savages because they know they can be impolite without having their skulls split.

The secret of your success is found in your daily routine.

Any 'free time' you have as an adult is actually just you postponing something.

Suicide does not end the chances of life getting worse. It eliminates the possibility of it ever getting better.

You can't change the past, but you can still fuck up your future.

Instead of merely talking about your life goals, take action and make them a reality. Verbally expressing your intentions can sometimes lead to receiving validation from others. This gives you a sense of satisfaction without actually achieving your goals. For instance, instead of seeking validation by saying you'll write a book, write the book first and let the validation follow afterwards.

Shopping is cheaper than a psychiatrist.

The scientific method is the most reliable way of understanding the natural world.

If you are reading this, you have survived up until this point. You went through who-knows-what, and you are still here. You are awesome.

Scientists don't know why, but you will find true love when you win the lottery.

Life is not defined by the events that occur, but rather by our reactions to them. Consider responding with a positive outlook.

Never sign a contract for an apartment you have not seen with your own eyes. Smell and noise do not show in pictures.

What triggers you, controls you. Let go.

If you do it right, it will last forever.

We are all bad in someone's story.

If you have trouble with your graphics in Windows, try Win + Ctrl + Shift + B. This will restart the graphics driver and might solve your problem.

Time alone is often a privilege. Don't waste it.

Don't hide it anymore. Drag it out into the open and make everyone look at it.

Never have your rules set in stone; the day you have to break them, you will break your own self.

Every entrepreneur was first an amateur.

With every decision you make, ask if it supports the life you are trying to create.

Jobs fill your pockets, adventures fill your soul.

Starve the ego, feed the soul.

What doesn't kill you only makes you weirder and harder to relate to.

Avoid making purchases if you don't have the means to cover at least three times the cost.

Bored? Create a playlist. Organize old photos. Craft something. Play a video game. Take a bath. Do a crossword puzzle. Learn something new. Dance. Make up a story. Declutter. Have sex. Lift weights. Stretch. Take a nap. Call a friend. Meditate. Read a Book. Cook or bake. Compose a song. Paint a picture. Go for a run.

One of the healthiest habits is to take nothing personally.

You are not your childhood trauma. You are not your high school trauma. You are not your parents. You are not your siblings. You are not your ex-relationships. You are not your failures. You are not poor choices you made. You are not the victim. Your past does not define you. You have the power to learn and grow. You can heal from anything in life. You get to define who you are. You get to decide who you are. You write your own story.

Moving fast ain't the goal. Moving correctly is.

Drink water. Get sunlight. You are basically a house plant with more complicated emotions.

The cat owns the house. That's why the word 'homeowner' has 'meow' in it.

Life shrinks or expands in proportion to one's courage.

Let each thing you would do, say, or intend, be like that of a dying person.

Don't waste your energy and money in nightclubs, unless you're tall, handsome, and wealthy (then you actually have a chance of enjoying this type of place). Instead, channel your time and finances into a hobby that genuinely adds value to your life.

People who think the environment is less important than the economy should try holding their breath while counting their money.

Nobody will stop you from creating. Do it today. Do it tomorrow. It's a way to make your soul grow, whether there is a market for it or not.

Be yourself. And while being yourself, make sure that you don't become full of yourself.

One that values the outer, soon becomes an outsider to ones own inner.

Go to school, get a job, go to work, get married, have some kids, pay your taxes, pay your bills, watch TV, listen to the news, obey the law. And then tell yourself that you are free.

Censorship is the tool used when the lie loses its power.

'Ctrl + F5' or 'Ctrl + R' reloads the webpage in your browser.

We all have the responsibility to consider others, including future generations.

Count your orgasms, not your calories.

Don't help someone who makes the same mistakes over and over.

Those not learning from history are doomed to repeat it. Those preventing history from being taught, intend to repeat it. Who controls the past, controls the future.

You don't have to be great to get started, but you have to get started to be great.

Sex is like poker. If you don't have a good partner, you better have a good hand.

Don't put any time into people that aren't interested.

The secret to happiness is really simple. Don't marry a bitch or an asshole.

Stop consuming sodas. Over time, they damage your teeth, joints, and your stomach.

Don't try to engineer a well-designed and well-functioning product on the first try. Don't fear imperfection; feel free to iterate. The right thing will emerge out of those iterations.

Be the kind of person who says 'Hi' to dogs.

If you don't have a plan, you become a part of someone else's plan.

Don't build second systems, look up the 'Second System Effect' and avoid it like the plague.

Attract what you expect. Reflect what you desire. Become what you respect. Mirror what you admire.

It's not prejudice if you call it religion.

Some people just need a high-five. In the face. With a chair.

Do it. We are not here for long.

Remove negative people from your life.

Vibes speak louder than words.

Write 'will you marry me?' in the sand.
It will fuck up someone's holiday.

If you work outdoors during the winter, there's no shame in investing in a pair of leggings. They're cost-effective and will help keep you warm.

What is meant to be will always find a way.

Slow is smooth, and smooth is fast.

You are judged by the company you keep.

Take it easy. Fuck your job, money is fake, society isn't natural and the sun is going to explode.

Boots first, then corset.

Never put cologne on your private parts.

The real luxuries in life are slow mornings, freedom to choose, a good night's sleep, peace of mind, calm days, people you love, people who love you, and being present.

One of life's biggest tragedies is that we get old too soon and wise too late.

Learn the difference between a reason and an excuse.

Your first 'anything' will be bad, but you can't make your 100th without making your first. Put your ego aside and start.

You must respect yourself before others can respect you.

Don't make eye contact when eating a banana.

Love can only be given. Love can never be earned.

Forgiveness is divine, but never pay full price for a late pizza.

Police officers are doing their jobs, they are not your friends.

Never put a kid in Superman pajamas on the top bunk.

A speaker of truth has no friends.

Pi is an endless, never-repeating decimal. It contains every possible number combination. If you convert it into ASCII text, somewhere in its infinite sequence is the name of everyone you will ever love, the exact date, time, and way you will die, and the answers to all the big questions of life. If you turn it into a bitmap image, it holds a perfect picture of the first thing you saw when you were born, the last thing you'll see before you die, and all the moments, big and small, in between. It includes all information that has ever existed or will ever exist, the DNA of every living being. Everything is contained in the ratio of a circle's circumference to its diameter.

Going back to a simpler life is not a step backward.

It's only a crime if there is a victim.

If you ever have the opportunity to walk out of jail, walk out as soon as possible. Don't wait for a lawyer. Leave the jail first, then talk to the lawyer.

Your comfort zone will kill you.

You don't have to give in to this recent culture of people telling you they are offended and expecting you to give a fuck.

Never get a tattoo that you can't cover with a wedding dress. Try seeing the big picture before making a rash choice. Your life may change, and unfortunately, not all of your decisions will age well.

Don't marry a 10 out of 10 or you will constantly have to worry about them cheating on you.

Fail harder. You cannot be successful without failure.

Don't impulse-buy clothes. Find styles that fit you and never deviate too much from them.

Stop the small talk. Forget about 'what's up'. Talk about atoms, death, the meaning of life, faraway galaxies, aliens, sex, magic, intellect, the lies you've told, your flaws, your favorite scents, your childhood, what keeps you up at night, your insecurities, your fears, your joys, love.

Being an adult is like folding a fitted sheet.

No whining, and always be respectful. But break the rules once in a while.

Before you do anything, ask yourself: 'Would an Idiot do that?'
If the answer is 'yes', do not do that thing.

This too shall pass. Things won't be difficult forever.

Stars can't shine without darkness.

Get some professional cleaning products for cleaning your stove and your windows. You'll end up using much less of the product, and you will save money and time despite the initial investment.

Everything is okay as long as you can get away with it.

Those who are able to see beyond the shadows and lies of their culture will never be understood, let alone believed by the masses.

Loneliness is cured by doing something that makes you happy.

Beware of those who cannot tell 'God's will' from their own.

There are 13 minerals that are essential for human life, and they can all be found in beer. Stay healthy.

Never let the things you want make you forget the things you have.

Always comment your code. Just because you are smart enough to write it doesn't mean others are smart enough to understand it.

To survive is to find meaning in the suffering.

Hold yourself accountable. Hold others accountable. Too much slides by because no one speaks up.

If you believe you have an illness, get it fixed while you are young, and potentially on your parent's health plan.

People often say that motivation doesn't last. Well, neither does bathing. That's why you should do it often.

Traveling is the only thing you can buy that makes you richer.

Don't make promises in the happiest moments. Don't make bold decisions in the saddest times.

It's always better to buy from the farmer's market rather than from the supermarket. It's also a good way to get experience on how to check the freshness of vegetables for future reference.

Start saving some money. Doesn't matter if it's only a couple of coins a month. Just save.

A child can teach an adult three things: To be happy for no reason. To always be busy with something. To know how to demand with all its might that which it desires.

Live so that when your children think of love, truth, and integrity, they think of you.

Don't buy new furniture, especially not from cheap stores. Buy old designer furniture if possible as it will increase in value over time.

When dealing with standard corkscrew threads, such as lids for bottles, extensions for poles, and screws, nuts, bolts, etc., always keep in mind 'righty tighty, lefty loosey'.

A society grows great when old men plant trees whose shade they know they shall never sit in.

To save money on Christmas gifts, be sure to bring up politics at Thanksgiving.

Let nature be your religion and earth be your church.

We are what we repeatedly do. Excellence is not an act. It's a habit.

If you need to show off with something, show off with how centered and balanced you are. Just buying crap to state your existence tells everyone that you haven't got a clue about happiness.

Be nice and kind to people. Everyone is fighting a fight, you know nothing about.

Raise your children to be impressed by kindness, loyalty, and humility, not by wealth, possessions and power.

We are our energy, not our age.

Never assume that a person of peace is unskilled at war.

Spend time with family and friends as often as you can; they will not be around forever.

You have to live your change.

There comes a time in life, when you walk away from all the drama and people who create it. Surround yourself with people who make you laugh, forget the bad, and focus on the good. Love the people who treat you right. Pray for the ones who don't.

The words you speak become the house you live in.

When you marry, you start having sex with a family member.

Life is too short to be anything but happy. Falling down is a part of life; getting back up is living.

If you work harder, quicker, and better at your job, you'll only bring more work onto yourself. Being smart at work is the key.

If you're lost at sea, don't drink ocean water. Try to distill it to remove the salt.

One 18-inch (45 cm) pizza has more 'pizza' than two 12-inch (30 cm) pizzas.

Be private, vibe alone, grow in silence.

If you're striving to eat healthier, but often forget about the vegetables in your fridge until they spoil, chop the veggies into bite-sized pieces and store them in a food-safe container. Or pack them into freezer bags and store them in the freezer. This way, you can quickly use the fresh vegetables as ingredients for various dishes or as snacks. The frozen ones can be used for sauce-based meals like lasagna or slow-cooker recipes. The same principle applies to fruits.

Using the Windows key in combination with the side arrow key will anchor the selected window to the edge of your screen. This is a quick method to set up a split-screen view.

Go where you feel most alive.

October is the best month to over-seed grass.

People who take the most pride in their race usually contribute the least to society.

If you get bullied, fight back. Always.

The whole universe is completely insane.

Buy some high-quality footwear. Your feet and your spine will appreciate it.

The thoughts you think and the way you feel are at the center of what you attract.

Life is half spent

before one knows what life is.

A bad system will beat a good person every time.

Slow down and enjoy the simple pleasures in life.

Train your mind to be stronger than your feelings.

If a candle falls over and wax is spilled on the carpet, wait till it's cooled, then take parchment paper, place it on the wax, and iron it out. The wax will stick to the paper.

Buy the dip. And never place a trade without a stop-loss order.

Your direction is more important than your speed.

Always be on the lookout for the presence of wonder.

Hire an accountant to do your taxes. It always pays off.

Everybody can be creative. Creativity is intelligence having fun.

He who scratches his butt should not pick his nose.

If you feel cold but your balls are still saggy, you might have a fever.

Male koalas don't chase females. They lay back, make themselves comfortable, and 'bellow' loudly at females in the area to come and join them.

Don't offer a lecture to a person who needs a hug.

Most people don't listen; they only wait for their turn to talk.

Be ambitious. Be hungry. Be driven.

To get rid of hiccups, take a deep breath and hold it for as long as you can.

Go to the dentist regularly. Make an appointment now if it has been more than six months since your last visit. Your future self will thank you.

The middle mouse button will open links in a new tab.

None of us sit high enough to look down on anyone.

Absurdity awakens the brain cells, and fantasy is an essential component of life.

There are only two days in the year where nothing can be done. One is called 'yesterday' and the other is called 'tomorrow'.

Too many of us sacrifice our creativity in order to do what we 'should do'.

In theory, there is no difference between theory and practice. In practice there is.

Be careful with what you hear about somebody; you might be hearing it from the problem.

Never eat in a place where the toilet is not clean.

If you are good at finding mistakes in others, you should also be good at correcting your own.

There is nothing quite as attractive as someone who listens not only to what you say, but also why you say it.

Find what you love and let it kill you.

Courage is knowing it might hurt, and doing it anyway. Stupidity is the same. And that's why life is hard.

Why do we only rest in peace? Why don't we live in peace too?

Whoever put the 'S' in fast-food was an absolute marketing genius.

You are not immune to propaganda. Many of the things you grew up believing to be true may be lies or misrepresentations.

If you have cats, check your bed for yakked-up hairballs before you get in.

Judging a person does not define who they are; it defines who you are.

Holding CTRL freezes the Windows Task Manager, allowing you to deal with programs constantly jumping around.

The shower curtain goes on the inside.

99% of all socks are single, and you don't see them crying about it.

Look for what you notice but no one else sees.

Sandpaper on orbital or rotary sanders lasts longer if you occasionally clean it with a brass brush.

Embody the change you wish to see in the world.

If you have mental stress, go outside and move. Our fight-or-flight instinct uses hormones to get us ready for a potentially dangerous situation. Moving will reduce these hormones and reduce the stress.

Old age comes at a bad time. When you finally know everything, you start to forget everything you know.

There is nothing more capitalist than a peanut with a top hat, cane, and a monocle selling you other peanuts to eat.

Blowing on the wine in your mug will help convince your Zoom meeting that your tea is hot.

Girls fuck who they want. Guys fuck who they can. Guys marry who they want. Girls marry who they can.

The reason you haven't found your soulmate yet may be that you don't have a soul.

If you feel like you are losing everything, remember, trees lose their leaves every year, yet they still stand tall and wait for better days to come.

Listen more to cautious older people with experience than to 'yolo' youngsters with ideas.

Put a dry towel into the dryer, and your clothes will dry faster.

Don't swim too close to the kid who is standing still in the pool.

If there was a button that we could push to get us everything we wanted, we would over-use it until everything we wanted lost all its value. Contrast is necessary.

Use oil on your knife before cutting an onion so you won't cry.

You can easily remove stickers from the windshield of your car with brake cleaner.

Don't marry if you're having second thoughts.

Invest in an Allen Wrench Drill Bit set. It will cut furniture-building time in half.

Don't fall for 'Limited time only' offers. If it sells out very quickly, there will be another offer, if it doesn't sell there will be an extension.

The G-spot is about 2-3 inches (5-8 cm) deep on the anterior wall.

Option-Shift-Command-V, paste and match style. It'll paste the item in the style of the place you copy it to, not the place you copied it from.

Apply a little bit of water to pizza that you want to reheat in the microwave. It will keep the pizza from getting spongy.

Understanding the 'drama triangle' is a great advantage at any workplace.

Never lend money to friends.

'Thoughts and prayers' is American slang for 'tough shit'.

Be yourself even when everyone is watching.

If you feel like you hate everyone: eat. If you feel like everyone hates you: sleep. If you feel like you hate yourself: shower. If you feel like everyone hates everyone: go outside.

Eat before you shop for groceries.

Try to go 24 hours without complaining, not even once. See how your life starts changing.

What other people think of you is none of your business.

Learn how to grow food. The ability to grow your own sustenance might be a lifesaver one day. Don't rely too heavily on grocery stores; even your balcony or windowsills can yield fruits and veggies.

Be professional. Be proficient. Be patient. Be present. Be persistent. Be particular. Be prevalent. Be prompt. Be prepared. Be poignant. Be profound. Be polite. Be poised. Be purposeful. Be passionate. Be practical. Be provocative. Be prosperous. Be peaceable. Be productive. Be perceptive. Be persuasive. Be pioneering. Be pliable. Be potent. Be practiced. Be precise. Be proactive. But don't try to be perfect.

Take a photo of every technical thing before you dismantle it.

If it's working, don't change it.

Collecting stuff is essentially a compensation for prior disappointment and an illusory comfort in the face of an uncertain future.

It's never about forgetting. It's about accepting and moving on.

Never treat a lady like an object. It hates that.

Before you get married, consider that a beautiful face will age and that a perfect body will change over time, but a beautiful soul will always be a beautiful soul.

Purchase a simple lock-picking set and practice a bit. It's a lot of fun and a great skill to have.

Sometimes people will act like you're hard to deal with because you aren't easy to fool.

Creative people need time to sit around and do nothing.

Perfect does not exist.

You have two lives. The second one begins when you realize you only have one.

You can prevent sneezing by pushing your tongue forcefully against your palate.

The closer we get to programming life-like simulations, the lower is the mathematical chance that we live in 'base-reality'. There is a very high probability that we are living in a simulation.

You are personally responsible for cleaning up your vibration and becoming an energetic match to the life you have been asking for.

Sometimes you can stop a nosebleed by pushing your finger on the middle part where the nose and upper lip meet.

Your triggers are your responsibility. It is not the world's obligation to tiptoe around you.

Make it happen. Shock everyone.

Tablets were replaced by scrolls.

Scrolls were replaced by books.

Today we scroll through books on tablets.

Don't trust people with visible missing teeth.

Microtransaction, or transgender midgets having sex.

The question is not what you look at, but what you see.

You can rub walnuts onto damaged wooden furniture to cover up marks.

You don't have to be extreme. Just consistent.

Question everything.

Time doesn't actually exist. Clocks exist. Time is just an agreed upon construct. We have taken a distance, one rotation of the earth, and one orbit of the sun, divided it up into segments, then given those segments labels. While it has its uses, we have been programmed to live our lives by this construct as if it were real. We have confused our shared construct with something that is tangible and thus have become its slaves.

Body lotion makes great leather conditioner.

Be an encourager. The world has plenty of critics.

The key to a good orgy is the catering.

Everything starts with you. You have the power to change today. You are responsible for your life.

Honor your emotions, but always choose to dwell on the positive ones.

You can. End of story.

Take your pleasure seriously.

If the steering wheel shakes while you are on the highway, you might need a wheel alignment.

Taking back your ex is like shoving toothpaste back into the tube.

Pussy is everywhere. Dick is everywhere. Chemistry isn't.

If you ask an airport employee to announce, 'a friend of Bill W. is requested to come to (your location)', it is very likely that a recovering alcoholic (member of Alcoholics Anonymous) will arrive to talk with you. Recovering alcoholics frequently find themselves craving a drink so badly that they need another alcoholic to talk to and work through it. 'Friends of Bill W.' are members of AA.

You never own an iPhone or an Android phone. Apple and Google simply let you use it; it always belongs to them.

Things change and friends leave. Life doesn't stop for anybody.

The greatest mistake in seduction is being too nice.

Knowing yourself is the beginning of all wisdom.

A dick has a sad life. His hair is a mess. His family is nuts. His neighbor is an asshole. His best friend is a pussy, and his owner beats him all the time.

You are doing better than you think.

When it feels scary to jump, that's exactly when you jump. Otherwise, you end up staying in the same place your whole life.

When you don't have a job, your job is to find a job. If you spend less than 40 hours a week searching you are not taking it seriously enough.

20 years from now, the only people who will remember that you worked late are your kids.

Try. Otherwise, you will never know.

Do a little dance. Make a little love. Get down tonight.

It will hurt more to remember opportunities that you did not have the courage to take than to remember failing. Take the chances, don't waste your time.

Before a date, masturbate.

We define love the way we experienced it.

If you get bitten by a mosquito, cut a garlic in half and rub it on the bite, it will numb your skin and stop the itching.

If you make any business deal with someone close to you, may it be friends or family, make sure to have airtight paper work.

Your inner peace has to be your priority. Do what you can to maintain it.

A well-built physique is a status symbol. It reflects you worked hard for it. No money can buy it. You cannot inherit it. You cannot steal it. You cannot borrow it. You cannot hold on to it without constant work. It shows dedication. It shows discipline. It shows self-respect. It shows dignity. It shows patience, work ethic, and passion.

Speak with honesty. Think with sincerity. Act with integrity.

Make people feel welcome, seen, and heard. The kindest thing you can do for another person is to show them that they matter.

Unconditional love does not mean unconditional tolerance.

Women know. They just know. Even if they didn't, they would still know. Men won't get this, but women will. Because they know.

This is your life. Do what you love, and do it often.

You can't help others if you haven't cared for yourself first.

Keep breathing and let life's experiences shape you.

Do it for you. Not for them.

Sometimes you are the dog, sometimes the tree.

The cold water is the knob on the right.

No matter how educated, talented, rich, or cool you think you are, what ultimately defines you is how you treat people.

Believe in yourself. And aliens.

You are allowed to change the price of what it costs to access you.

Mental health first: learn how your brain works and don't follow generic 'this thing makes you feel better' advice. We are all different and have different needs.

When your boss or client is explaining what they want, listen to every detail before making any plan in your head. If you do not pay full attention and later ask for something they already said, it will give a negative impression of you.

Any book worth banning is worth reading.

Live simply. Love big. Calm down. Work hard. Be kind.

To err is human; to arr is pirate.

You can use a laundry clip as a toothbrush stand.

Learn to lay back and to observe. It's okay to not always have an opinion on everything.

If people are doubting how far you can go, go so far you can't hear them anymore.

We all deserve a beach break.

Appreciate and learn from both sides.

Tell the people you love that you love them. You never know when they will be gone forever.

You can always block, mute, or quit social media.

The only intelligent, tactical response to life's horror is to laugh defiantly at it.

Women fall in love by what they hear. Men fall in love by what they see. That's why women wear makeup and men lie.

States, churches, nations, rank, ideology, prices: they all solely exist within the realm of human perception and belief. Understand the distinction between objectively existing things, and things existing only for some.

Real is more attractive than perfect.

There are bosses, and then there are leaders.

Everything will be ok. There are much dumber people out there and they are doing just fine.

If you're going to do something, do it well or not at all.

Less drama. More karma.

Hugging your people is what makes any place home.

A project manager is a person who thinks nine women can deliver a baby in one month.

The cure for boredom is curiosity.

Hail Sithis.

A real man doesn't feel happiness. Just less anger.

Focus on your own shit to be successful.

Be the light that darkness fears.

This page. Nice.

You don't have to be like the rest of them, darling.

Everyone is fighting battles you don't know about, so be kind.

You will save a lot of time and money if you own a tool chest and learn how to fix things. YouTube is a great source.

Real intimacy is when you can be weird and have unfiltered conversations together.

Be as you wish to seem.

If the people don't find you handsome, they should at least find you handy or funny.

Always get your wife a snack at the gas station, even if you think that she doesn't want a snack. Get the woman a snack.

Mages call it spells. Christians, Jews, and Muslims call it prayer. Spiritualists call it manifestation. Atheists call it the placebo effect. Scientists call it quantum physics. Everyone is arguing over its name. No one is denying its existence.

People say you don't need alcohol to have fun. The thing is, you also don't need shoes to run, but it definitely makes it easier.

Make a financial spreadsheet for yourself, so you know how much money you spend and for what. Its a tremendous help to know just how much money you actually need each month.

Patience is a form of action. But remember: your time is limited.

The revolution starts at home.

If you spent less time bitching about your life, you'd possibly enjoy it more.

Don't judge people for their choices when you don't understand their reasons.

Your energy is currency. Spend it well, invest it wisely.

The nine noble virtues are: courage, truth, honor, fidelity, discipline, hospitality, self-reliance, industriousness, and perseverance.

Wonder and you might get lost.

Never think of yourself as being useless. You can always be used as a bad example.

The smarter you become, the sadder you get, unless you understand not to give a fuck.

The grass is not greener somewhere else. The grass is green where you water it.

Try to figure out what you really want in life as soon as possible. Without a goal or at least a direction, you might end up in a situation you don't like and which could have been avoided.

Consistency is more important than perfection.

There will always be someone who can't see your worth. Don't let it be you.

Don't ever touch your work laptop or phone when you are drunk. Don't answer to anyone when you are drunk, especially if you are frustrated with that person. No matter how good your reply might sound, never hit that send button.

The best way to keep a prisoner from escaping is to make sure they never know they are in prison.

Solitude over toxicity.

Either you run the day, or the day runs you.

If you wouldn't like it done to you, don't do it to others.

Learn to be self-sufficient.

Breathe in slowly, hold for four seconds. Breathe out and relax your shoulders.

If routine and mundane chores like laundry, cleaning, and dishwashing start sparking conflicts between you and your partner, consider outsourcing as much of it as possible. Invest in a robotic vacuum to handle the dust, a floor cleaner for wet-cleaning, or a dishwasher if you don't already have one.

Nothing is really lost until your mom can't find it.

Six months of focus and alignment can put you five years ahead in life.

The best part of a cucumber tastes like the worst part of a watermelon.

Incorporate short breaks into your workday. If your colleagues take cigarette breaks, even if you don't smoke, consider joining them or taking a break on your own. Ensure you step away from indoor lighting and screens for five minutes every hour if possible.

People don't fake depression; they fake being okay. Be kind.

No matter how much you don't want to do something, sometimes necessity takes over. Be ready.

Choose a good partner who's smart. They all have genitals.

Abuse of power comes as no surprise.

Sleep more than you study. Study more than you party. But party as much as you can.

Never go through a breakup or quit your job during PMS week.

Don't underestimate the power of consistency.

Better shit and be late than shit yourself in a meeting.

If you have cats, check the washing machine before turning it on.

One of the hardest lessons in life is letting go. Whether it's guilt, anger, love, loss or betrayal, ultimately, we all have to let go.

Never reply to hate messages. Don't negotiate with terrorists.

When you are thinking about your life, remember that no amount of guilt can change the past, and no amount of anxiety can change the future.

It is so simple to be happy, but so difficult to be simple.

Learn how to use your Mac's command line; it is basically a powerful Unix shell.

It's better to look back on life and say 'I can't believe I did that' than to look back and say 'I wish I did that'.

Don't forget about your dreams. Keep sharpening your talents. Hold on to your ambition. You did not peak. You are just getting started.

Take the break you think you don't have the time for.

Don't touch your private parts after chopping chili.

The next best way to solving a problem is finding some humor in it.

Sometimes, turning it off and on again works wonders.

If you can't be kind, be quiet.

Check your testicles. Check them regularly and have them checked by a professional once a year, especially if you are over 40.

If you are going to buy anything that is not within your budget, imagine it on one hand and the money it costs on the other hand. If you feel it will ease your daily life, buy it. If it's just a craving, put that shit back on the shelf.

Delete the drama.

People will love you. People will hate you. None of it will have anything to do with you.

Never marry someone without living together for a few months or even years. Experience not just the fun bits like dates, sex, and fancy restaurants, but things like shared money, grocery shopping, morning breath, cleaning chores etc.

Be nice, until it's time to not be nice.

If you are ever struggling with a decision, ask yourself what Star Trek's Spock would do.

Texting is a brilliant way to miscommunicate how you feel, and misinterpret what other people mean.

Just do it. Sometimes, all it takes is that extra push to get started, and you'll find that the rest of the journey is far smoother than you expected.

If they cheat on somebody to be with you, they will probably cheat on you to be with somebody else.

Stop making stupid people famous. Stop following idiots.

Never give unsolicited advice. Keep it to yourself.

Ctrl, Alt, Del. Control yourself. Alter your way of thinking. Delete negativity.

Never participate in a battle that someone else orchestrated.

Kettles can not only be used to heat up water for tea. You can also cook eggs and sausages in a kettle.

Know who you are and just be it. That's where all your power lies.

Whenever you are in the position to help someone, be glad and always do it because that's the universe answering someone's prayers through you.

Keep your head high and your middle finger higher.

Don't put wicker trash cans in your bathroom.

When looking back doesn't interest you anymore, you are doing something right.

Don't be too busy to see that your day might be full of magic.

Intentionally be the best version of you.

Outgrow your own bullshit.

The world is not full of assholes, but they are so strategically placed that you get to see one every day.

Almost all hardship and ordeals will have an ending. Be steadfast, be strong. Don't give up or make stupid decisions in the moment. There is usually light at the end of the tunnel. You will become much wiser and stronger.

If you procrastinate a lot, set yourself a ridiculously small goal. It will get you started, and it's better than doing nothing.

Be more interested in how your life feels than how it looks to others.

Act without expectation.

In the end, everything will be okay. If it's not okay, it's not the end.

Surround yourself with people who talk about visions and ideas.

Control your level of empathy. It's a fine line between caring and being taken advantage of.

You can pick your friends, and you can pick your nose. But you shouldn't pick your friend's nose.

None of the social media shit matters. Be a solid and good person in real life.

The secret to having it all is knowing you already do.

If you're thinking about cutting your nails, do it.

The brain controls every muscle in the body, except for the heart. That has a mind of its own.

All sorts of things in this world behave like mirrors.

Laugh more.

Don't let the success of others make you feel bad. Envy is a bitch, and you never know what others go through.

We learn by imitation, so be careful who you're trying to imitate.

Music melts all the separate parts of our bodies together.

Comparison will kill you.

Turn off the 'news' and love your neighbor.

Manifesting or vocalizing your desires allows the world to align itself with your thoughts.

Stop worrying about what other people think. Have you seen other people? They're awful.

You need a little bit of insanity to do great things.

You can go to the gym, drink your water, and take your vitamins, but you have to deal with what's going on in your heart and head as well to be healthy.

Time is not refundable; use it with intention.

The problem with capitalism is that if you are not born into wealth, your only capital is your labor. So automatically, your body is a commodity that you must sell, and if you can't sell it for enough, you won't be able to care for it, and you will lose your only capital.

Things of quality have no fear of time.

Turning your phone's data connection on and off during a call can sound like you are having a problem with the signal, in case you want to end a call early.

Heart-shaped chocolates go on huge sales after Valentines Day. The same goes for Christmas chocolates after Christmas.

A wise person learns from their mistakes. A wiser person learns from the mistakes of others.

Dream so big you can't fall asleep at night.

Wash your hands with cold instead of hot water after chopping garlic.

The things you look at change, if you change the way you look at things.

Take a deep breath in through your nose. Count to four. Breathe out.

It should be chronicled for future generations that every country with nuclear weapons and other lethal means of ending the world many times over were short on ventilators, medicine, doctors, and hospital staff when a pandemic hit.

Having a good heart can put you in some fucked-up situations.

If you are dating someone, try and find out how that person was raised. A lot of people weren't raised on love; they were raised on survival. A person's past affects how they look at life.

Bad communication ends a lot of good things.

Marry the one who loves you, not the one you hope will love you.

Praise in public. Correct in private.

The world needs more tackle boxes and fewer Xboxes.

Make a point of walking barefoot in the grass every once in a while.

The six biggest doctors in the world are sun, rest, exercise, diet, self-respect, and friends. Stick to them at all stages in your life.

In the blink of an eye, it can all vanish. Be grateful, always.

If your dad tells you to pull his finger, don't.

Don't try and change your partner if it isn't working. Do both of you a favor and move on.

Time is precious; waste it on something you love.

Make art or die trying.

You don't buy things with money; you buy them with hours of your life.

A healthy relationship is one where two independent people just make a deal that they will help make the other person the best version of themselves.

Boobs are to men

what laser pointers are to cats.

A lot of people become unattractive once you find out how they think.

Sometimes all it takes is one slow-walking person in the supermarket to destroy the illusion of being a nice person.

Don't believe everything you think.

When a shaky 10-year-old puts a gun in your face, do whatever the fuck they say.

See how fast the last year passed? You better do what you want to do now.

It's ok to disappear until you find yourself again.

You can't just hope for happy endings. You have to believe in them, do the work, and take the risks.

At a certain age, you can never be sure if you actually have free time or if you just keep forgetting things.

Nothing is for free; there's a price for everything. You either choose your own way of paying, or life will choose for you.

Meditation is a lifesaver.

What is done with love is done well.

You can't drink the whole day, if you don't start in the morning.

People talk of God or fate when they don't know who fucked them over.

This planet is probably used by other planets as a lunatic asylum.

A relationship is like a house. When a lightbulb burns out, you don't go and buy a new house; you fix the lightbulb.

You can't get the word back after it's said, the occasion after it's missed and the time after it's gone.

Get out of bed running, or sooner or later, you will be crawling out crying.

Help and treat yourself like it's someone else you care about.

Enter every room with the energy of a cat. 'Is there anything I can fuck up or eat in here? Nah? Well anyway, you're lucky to have me.'

Hurt people hurt people.

When a clown moves into a palace, he doesn't become a king. The palace becomes a circus.

If your doctor prescribes you medication without first asking about your diet, you sleep, your exercise routine, your water consumption, whether you have any structural issues, and the stress in your life, then you don't have a doctor; you have a drug dealer.

You can learn a lot from your mistakes when you are not busy denying them.

Don't make yourself small for anyone. Ever. Be the awkward, funny, intelligent, beautiful little weirdo that you are. Don't hold back.

20 minutes of doing something is more valuable than 20 hours of thinking about doing something.

Dance like everyone else can go fuck themselves.

A good travel towel is one of the most useful things to have.

When times are weird, focus on what you can control.

Good conversation starters are asking questions like: What sorts of things make you laugh? Do you have any pet peeves? Have you ever had a nickname, and what was the story behind it? What are some of the items on your bucket list? What is your favorite childhood memory, and what made it special for you? Who is your celebrity crush, and why? What is your favorite cartoon? What would be your superhero name? If you could trade lives with anybody for a day, who would it be? What countries have you travelled to? Do you like to cook and what is your favorite dish?

Glass half empty or half full, you will still not die of thirst.

It's only a waste of money if you get no value from it.

You weren't born to just pay bills and die.

Love your job, but don't love your company, because you never know when your company might stop loving you.

When you let the people do what they want, you get Woodstock. When you let governments do what they want, you get Auschwitz.

The best way to get a right answer on the internet is not to ask a question; it is to post a wrong answer.

Don't ever make life-changing decisions when you are sad, happy, or drunk. Wait until you are serene.

If you're deep in mud, calm down and move slowly.

You can use hammer mode on your drill to actually hammer nails.

You can turn your sofa into a bed simply by telling your wife to calm down.

You can not grow if you are bitter.

Computers, cellphones, and tablets are good, but they are like candy-good. A bit once in a while is okay, but don't overdo it. A book, pen and paper, a walk, sports, a hobby are good like potatoes-good. They will feed your life.

Don't make friends out of your coworkers.

We should not teach kids that being naughty or nice determines the gifts you receive in life. Be nice for the sake of being a decent human being, or be a dick because sometimes people deserve it. And if you want cool presents, buy your own shit.

Masturbate before making a big decision. Post-nut clarity is a real thing.

Don't put the food in the center of the plate in a microwave. It will heat much faster if it is distributed evenly. Also, make sure that the plate rotates in the microwave.

Going cheap often becomes very expensive.

Only dumb people take drugs; the smart people are the ones selling them. Same goes for banks and robbers. Only dumb people rob banks; smart crooks are operating them.

Never invest all your savings. Only invest what you can afford to lose.

Remember the magic words: 'please', 'thank you' and 'step off, bitch'.

If anything in a relationship is bothering you, don't ignore it. Try to resolve it as soon as possible. Communication is key.

Rest is not a reward. You don't have to earn rest. You need rest. You deserve rest. You are worthy of rest simply because you are a living being. Don't ever feel guilty for taking time to rest.

Never date someone that has less to lose than you.

If you realized how powerful your thoughts are you would never think a negative thought again.

We should make dogs wear costumes more often. They already don't know what's going on; why wait for a holiday.

If you lend money to a friend and they start avoiding you, that's the amount it cost you to get rid of that fake friend.

Never compliment a woman on her mustache, no matter how impressive it may be.

Don't worry about not having your dream job yet, life is not a race.

Take it easy; you will get there.

Shit happens, so keep a pack of baby wipes handy.

Find a person who tells you to 'keep fucking going' when you feel discouraged instead of asking you 'are you done yet'. This support should apply to hobbies, career aspirations, and sex positions.

Change your mind when presented with a good argument. You are under no obligation to be the same person you were an hour ago.

Don't do good for people more than you should. Their expectations grow and you won't be able to keep up.

If you feel the majority of people are idiots, chances are you are also an idiot.

You are the greatest project you will ever work on.

One life. Just one. Why aren't we running towards our wildest dreams like we are on fire?

Learn some basic dance moves to dance with a partner, no matter if it is salsa, waltz, or foxtrot. Own those moves and be a good guide to your partner when you dance.

Marry your best friend.

Knowledge is power. Whenever the opportunity to acquire knowledge arises, seize it. You never know when, how, or for whom it might prove valuable. If you choose knowledge solely based on its immediate utility, you might never be able to come up with an original idea or solution to a problem.

Self-care is not a luxury; it's a must.

You don't need someone who sees the good in you. You need someone who sees the bad and still wants you.

Expect hardship, forgive, and try harder. Everyone faces challenges.

If you start your own company, remember: people join because of great vision, and people leave because of poor leadership.

Find something to do that you love. There is no guarantee for a happy and long retirement.

Dress well and take care of your body. It's a form of good manners.

Do yoga. It's great for your body and your mental health.

If you are on the dance-floor and you think a person likes you because they look in your direction, relocate. If they scan the floor for you, you'll know for sure.

Adults are just kids in grown-up costumes.

Everyone appreciates your honesty, until you are honest with them. Then you are an asshole.

You can avoid reality, but you cannot avoid the consequences of avoiding reality.

Get your prostate checked early. It's much more comfortable than going through chemotherapy.

Spit on toilet paper to turn it into a wet-wipe.

It ain't what you don't know that gets you into trouble. It's what you think you know for certain, that just isn't like you thought it was.

People don't want to hear your opinion. They want to hear their opinion coming out of your mouth.

Dreaming, after all, is a form of planning.

If you're on a date with someone, and they leave their phone on the table, you might want to move on.
If they can't invest an hour of their undivided attention, what will the rest of the relationship look like?
Humanity has endured for millennia without needing constant minute-by-minute updates on everyone's lives. If there is a genuine emergency, texting from a restaurant won't necessarily resolve it.

When in doubt, take a nap.

If you ever experience any facial trauma resulting in one of your eyes appearing droopy, don't ignore it. Head to your nearest hospital, as this could be a sign of an orbital blowout fracture. Seek medical attention promptly.

You can add a '+' and numbers to the end of your gmail address and emails will still reach your inbox. For example, if your email address is 'myname@gmail.com' you can use 'myname+123@gmail.com'. That way it is easy to see who is selling your address and it's easy to block spam mail going to that address.

Attraction is incredibly diverse and goes beyond just physical appearance and wealth. Most people seek stability and positive qualities in a partner. Don't pursue individuals who desire what you lack. Focus on being a stable and genuine person with positive traits.

Windows key + Shift + S lets you take screenshots quickly.

Learn to shut the fuck up. It's not as easy as it sounds, but learn to shut up. It will save you a lot of money and nerves down the road.

A bad day of fishing beats a hard day's work.

The only way out is through.

How you speak to yourself matters.

No matter how good the hand soap smells, never come out of a restroom smelling your fingers.

The answers to your questions may not be at the beach, but you should at least check.

Your partner should make your dick hard, not your life. Or your pussy wet, and not your eyes.

You are most likely overthinking. You got this.

If you have dark circles under your eyes, eat a lot of junk and stay up all night. If you are small and chubby, and cute, but will put up a fight, you might be a raccoon.

Remember when you wanted what you currently have.

If it's very hot outside and you need to drive somewhere, take a bottle of water and a hat with you. If your car breaks down, you won't have air conditioning, and you might need to wait for help outside the car, possibly in the sun.

Sex is foremost a mental thing. Make the mind lose it, and the body will follow.

Look at your desktop. All these open windows, but no fresh air.

The best thing about having a penis is sharing it with people who don't. The same goes for vaginas and boobs.

Don't be too shy to say 'yes', and never afraid to say 'no'.

Begin. Even if you have no idea if it will work.

Shop for ingredients you've never used before and look up possible recipes after you buy them. You might discover new food you like.

It's not hoarding if your stuff is cool.

Schools at night, leaving the movie theater late, empty beaches early in the morning, and traffic lights when there are no cars around late at night, are all places where reality seems altered.

One man's trash is another man's treasure.

Hugging and cuddling are very good for your health. Do it often.

Concern should drive us into action, and not into depression.

Beware of the human-shaped drugs. The detox is a painful one.

If a cat is coming towards you with a bit of a swagger, don't pet it.

Be more like Jesus. Hang out with sinners. Upset religious people. Tell stories that make people think. Choose unpopular friends. Be kind, loving, and merciful. Take naps on boats.

Time is an illusion. Lunchtime doubly so.

Happiness is reality minus expectations.

Deviation from the norm will be punished unless it is exploitable.

Ignorance can be educated. Crazy can be medicated. But there is no cure for stupid.

In the future, everyone will want to be anonymous for fifteen minutes.

Never say never. A lot of things you think will never happen, will indeed happen.

If someone is addicted to masturbating but then gets addicted to sex, it is fair to say that their addiction got out of hand.

It's not 'science' if you can't question it.

Modern education is creating people smart enough to follow orders and repeat what they are told, and dumb enough to think this makes them smarter than everyone else.

Reality is for people who can't handle drugs.

Fear is a liar.

Shine without the desire to be seen.

Never forget your traditions; they'll keep you grounded.

If you can make a person laugh, you're almost there.

Life is too short to learn from your own mistakes.

Make yourself proud, but beware of your own expectations.

Sometimes what is left unsaid, says it all.

Healthy food such as peppers, potatoes, apples, squash, cabbage, cucumber, herbs, spices, and grains can last months if stored properly at a temperature of 40-50 degrees Fahrenheit (4-10 degrees Celsius), in a dark basement or cellar.

To exit the Vi or Vim editor, press Esc a few times, then type :q! and press Enter.

To produce a nice sound on a violin, you have to make sure that the bow is parallel to the bridge.

Popular entertainment is basically propaganda for the status quo.

Do. Not. Hate. When anger boils in you about something that you can do nothing about, it tends to coalesce into a hate. Hate will cost you time, health, and in some cases, even friends. Forgive yourself for getting into whatever made you hate, and leave it behind.

In the age of information, ignorance is a choice.

Success is never owned; it is rented and the rent is due every day.

Book a vacation so you have something to look forward to.

Sometimes you just have to sit in the car and let the song finish.

Never take a laxative and a sleeping pill at the same time.

Always pay attention while driving on the road. We tend to doze off in familiar places because we know them. Most car accidents happen close to home.

Discover who you are by acting naturally.

The deer isn't crossing the road. The road is crossing the forest.

You never really lived until you've nearly died.

Instead of looking at your phone all the time, you could make some art. Kiss someone. Read a book. Cut up old magazines. See a friend. Write down your dreams. Do something you are bad at, or tell someone you love them.

Happiness is the new rich. Inner peace is the new success. Health is the new wealth. Kindness is the new cool.

'I bought this while I was depressed' should be an acceptable reason to get a full refund on a return.

If you want to buy something, wait two weeks, if you still want to buy it, it's probably something you need or just want really bad, so buy it. But if you forget about it, it's not that important and you saved your money.

Life is mostly just killing the time while you wait for it to shower you with meaning and happiness.

Sometimes to achieve success, you must, no matter how steep, take the first step.

The greatest enemy of truth is the illusion of knowledge. Your knowledge is only as good as the source of your information.

Practice media distancing.

Every minute you're not dead should be a minute spent enjoying the fuck out of life.

It takes seven seconds for food to pass from mouth to stomach. A human hair can hold about 3 kilograms or 6 pounds. The length of the penis is three times the length of the thumb. The femur is as hard as concrete. A woman's heart beats faster than a man's. Women blink two times as much as men. We use 300 muscles just to keep our balance when we stand. A woman has read this entire text. A man is still looking at his thumb.

If it comes, let it. If it goes, let it.

The sheep will spend its entire life fearing the wolf, only to be eaten by the shepherd.

If you want do something, you will find solutions. If you don't want to do it, you will find reasons. Inaction is the number one cause of failure. Therefore, measure progress rather than success or failure.

Can one be immoral and not know it?

Love, sex, and romance aren't enough for a fulfilling relationship. What really makes a relationship work is commitment, respect, good communication, a sense of humor, and doing more than your share of the work. Let go of grudges and be ready to compromise.

Whatever you're meant to do, do it now. The conditions are always impossible.

Everything we hear is an opinion, not a fact. Everything we see is a perspective, not the truth.

When you cook chicken breast, cut it in half to even the thickness. Cook it whole and not diced, the meat is done when it doesn't sink in but rather springs back.

Doing nothing is very different from having nothing to do.

Results happen over time, not overnight. Work hard, stay consistent, stay humble, be patient and never give up.

Marriage is like a deck of cards. In the beginning, all you need is two hearts and a diamond. By the end, you wish you had a club and a spade.

Being an adult is 90% stressing about money and 10% spending money you don't have on treats because you've worried a lot this week.

Sometimes miracles are just good people with kind hearts.

Orgasms are one of the healthiest forms of stress release. So, in the future, when you tell somebody to go fuck themselves, it is because you care.

There is no internet 'cloud'. It's just someone else's computer.

Spend plenty of time with the people you love. Value that time over anything else.

You need money because you are forced to exist on a planet which requires arbitrary pieces of paper to be exchanged for basic needs.

Be known for your kindness and grace.

One minute you're 21, staying up all night drinking beer, eating pizza, and doing sketchy stuff just for fun. Then, in the blink of an eye you're 50, drinking water, eating salad, and you can't do any sketchy stuff because you pulled a muscle putting on your socks.

If you can't change it, let it go. It's a waste of energy.

If they say it's safe, it's probably not.

A glove and two sponges go a long way.

Go to see the dentist as soon as you feel you might have a tooth issue. Unchecked dental problems will only get worse and can lead to other serious health issues.

Only the weak are cruel. Gentleness can only be expected from the strong.

Educate yourself. When a question about a certain topic pops up, search for it on the internet. Watch movies and documentaries. When something sparks your interest, read about it. Read, read, read. Study, learn, stimulate your brain. Educate that beautiful mind of yours.

Keep some spare bootlaces around if you work outside.

Try an activity that you liked, or were good at when you were younger.

The more you weigh, the harder you are to kidnap. Stay safe, eat cake.

If you are feeling down and tired, all you have to do is to completely fix your life so you can relax all the time and never have to think about anything.

You are the carbon they want to reduce.

Don't go shopping for food on an empty stomach.

Before you judge others or claim any absolute truth, consider that you can see less than 1% of the electromagnetic spectrum and hear less than 1% of the acoustic spectrum. As you read this, you are traveling at 220 kilometers per second across the galaxy. 90% of the cells in your body carry their own microbial DNA and are not 'you'. The atoms in your body are 99.999999999999% empty space, and none of them are the ones you were born with, but they all originated in the belly of a star. Human beings have 46 chromosomes, 2 less than the common potato. The existence of the rainbow depends on the conical photoreceptors in your eyes. To animals without cones, the rainbow does not exist. All the colors you see represent less than 1% of the electromagnetic spectrum.

Life without passion is a slow way to freeze to death.

The happiest people are the givers, not the takers.

Intuition is real. Vibes are real. Energy doesn't lie. Tune in.

Books are the most constant of friends, the most accessible and wisest of counsellors, and the most patient of teachers.

Choose wisely, where you spend your time and energy. If you died today, your company would hire someone new within a week but your family would miss you for the rest of their lives.

If you behaved like your government, you'd be arrested.

Opt for a career in the arts only if you're willing to wholeheartedly commit to it and can't envision doing anything else. It's advisable to have a plan B. Being a professional artist is an incredibly challenging path, and long-term satisfaction is often achieved only by the most dedicated individuals, with many leaving the field in their 30s.

Switching to your secondary weapon is faster than reloading.

Everything you want is on the other side of fear.

Being a pessimist and denying it by saying you are realistic, just makes your life much harder.

All we see or seem is but a dream within a dream.

In Excel, CTRL + : inserts the current date. CTRL + Shift + : inserts time

Bulbasaur is the best starter.

May your life be like a roll of toilet paper. Long and useful.

Sometimes you don't get what you want because you deserve better.

It's very healthy to spend time alone. You need to know how to be alone and not be defined by another person.

Salt your pasta water before boiling. The water should taste almost as salty as the ocean.

Learn about the scientific method. We could save ourselves a lot of discussions if we all had a baseline knowledge about how not to deceive oneself.

Never brake with your left foot.

The same boiling water that softens the potato, hardens the egg. It's about what you're made of, not the circumstances.

You can have results or excuses. Not both.

Don't let fear choose for you when making an important decision.

Laughing reduces the chance of heart disease, it is a natural painkiller. It improves breathing, helps you lose weight, and gives you a good sleep. It decreases stress and makes you look young.

You are a ghost, driving a meat-coated skeleton, made from stardust, riding a rock floating through space. Fear nothing.

Poking a campfire with a stick is one of life's greatest satisfactions.

Intelligent people tend to have fewer friends than the average person. The smarter you are, the more selective you become.

Never build on your in-law's land.

To keep warm in a sleeping bag on a cold night, shake up your bag. Do some jumping jacks and fuel up with a pre-bedtime snack. Don't sleep in your damp day clothes and wear dedicated wool socks if possible. Wear a hat and keep off the ground.

Measure twice, cut once.

Sometimes you have to wonder whether the world is being run by smart people taking the piss or by imbeciles who really mean it.

You will never find a companion that will be so companionable as solitude.

Before sex, you help each other get naked. After sex, you only dress yourself. Moral of the story: in life, no one helps you once you are fucked.

Simplicity is the ultimate sophistication. Strip away any unnecessary complexity.

A lot of people never heal, because they stay in their heads, replaying corrupted scenarios.

If it smells like a fish, it is a tasty dish. If it smells of cologne, leave it alone.

Binge drinking is like borrowing happiness from tomorrow.

You start with a full bag of luck and an empty bag of skill. The goal is to fill up the bag of skill before you empty the bag of luck.

If you want to achieve something, but you tend to procrastinate, use the 'pomodoro' technique. Set a kitchen timer to 25 minutes and see how much you can get done within this interval. Take a 5-minute break, then the next interval. The intervals will add up and you'll eventually reach your goal.

If you see a beautiful flower, sniff it. Stop and smell the roses every once in a while.

Don't let age change you. Change the way you age.

Don't just teach your children to read; teach them to question what they read. Teach them to question everything. The value of an education is not the learning of many facts, but the training of the mind to think.

Work hard, become rich, and then die anyway.

Life is like PVP pretending to be PVE.

If you find yourself busy with a partner and kids, set aside one hour twice a week for sports. Now, not in 10 years. Support each other in doing this. Your life will improve a lot.

The more you sweat in training, the less you bleed in combat.

Be passionate and be involved in what you believe in, and do it as thoroughly, honestly, and fearlessly as you can.

When you're 20, you care what everyone thinks. When you're 40, you stop caring what everyone thinks. When you're 60, you realize that no one was ever thinking about you in the first place.

Try to earn time for yourself in life, not money.

If you are going to quit anything, quit being lazy, quit making excuses, and quit waiting for the right time.

Forgive them once, and they'll get more cunning next time.

Being polite is so rare these days that it is often confused with flirting.

You don't need a 'happily ever after'. You need someone who makes you realize what matters. And sometimes that person will be a pain in the ass.

Do no harm, take no shit.

At age 4, success is not peeing in your pants. At age 12, success is having friends. At age 16, success is having a driver's license. At age 20, success is having sex. At age 35, success is having money. At age 50, success is having money. At age 60, success is having sex. At age 70, success is having a drivers license. At age 75, success is having friends. At age 80, success is not peeing in your pants.

By replacing your morning coffee with green tea, you can lose up to 90% of what little joy you still have left in your life.

If you can't make a friend, don't make an enemy.

Don't think of yourself as an ugly person. Think of yourself as a beautiful monkey.

Better to fight and fall than to live without hope.

The number one rule for every entrepreneur is: turnover is vanity, profit is sanity, cash is reality.

A lot of people have ovaries, so don't be mad when they are ovary-acting.

Do not allow the demons of anger or doubt to rule over you.

People can't read your thoughts, but they can read your reaction to statements and questions.

Do good, recklessly.

Greed is a mental illness.

Wake up with determination. Go to bed with satisfaction.

There is no age limit for building blanket forts.

One drink is too much and two drinks are not enough.

Surround yourself with people who bring you up, not down. Don't let anybody disturb your inner peace.

Sometimes an appropriate response to reality is to go insane.

If you don't want the magicians to fool you, don't go to the circus.

The act of creating something is always more important than the result.

Don't be afraid of losing people. We are born alone, we die alone.

To appear interesting to unfamiliar people, simply listen to them attentively and ask questions. In the end, the person may lead the conversation themselves, and they'll find you interesting because they're discussing a topic they enjoy. When seeking acceptance in a group, prioritize discussing others' interests before introducing your own.

We are all born ignorant, but one must work hard to remain stupid.

Be careful whose advice you take and be patient with those who supply it.

True warriors confront the evil that most people refuse to even admit exists.

If you do the following for 30 days you will be unrecognizable: sleep 8 hours a day, drink 2 liters of water daily, get some sun daily, no sugar, read for 30 minutes a day, workout three times a week, capture someone and cut their face off and sew it onto your face, meditate for 10 minutes daily.

Kissing is underrated.

If you have a craving for chocolate, you need magnesium which is found in nuts, seeds, veggies, and fruits.

Living alone has a lot of advantages. You can walk around naked all day and you don't have to talk to anybody. You can buy minimal groceries and no one drinks your leftover alcohol. You can sleep anywhere, clean up when you want, cook what you want, and sing out loud without having to explain why. Lazy days are real, and so is peace of mind.

Be who you want to be, not what others want to see.

Just because it's a bad idea doesn't mean it won't be a good time.

Sometimes we need fantasy to survive the reality.

Don't wait until you are ready. There is almost no such thing as ready. There is only now. And you may as well do it now. Generally speaking, now is as good a time as any.

No shortcuts. Work for it.

Keep the grinding at an absolute minimum.

Don't make big decisions on an empty stomach or full balls.

Take walks to ease or prevent anxiety.

Don't sweat for pounds, inches, or a dress size. Sweat to make your outside match your inside.

It is better to be a warrior in a garden than a gardener in a war.

Make sure your worst enemy doesn't live between your own two ears.

Whatever you are not changing, you are choosing. Read that again.

Life humbles us so deeply as we age. You realize how much nonsense you've wasted time on.

Graffiti keeps rents low.

Focus on yourself. Don't get lost in other people.

Everything you see on TV is a scripted performance for the purpose of shaping your worldview to benefit the powerful interests running the show. Operation Mockingbird is not a conspiracy theory.

The cake is a lie.

Be hot, be naughty, be courteous.

Computer games don't affect kids. If Pac-Man affected us as kids, we'd all be running around in darkened rooms, munching magic pills and listen to repetitive music.

A lot of what is real was imagined first.

It's better to face rejection for being true to yourself than to pretend and act like a doormat just to please someone.

We all just stumble through life's challenges.

Popularity is totally overrated.

You can't out-train a bad diet.

Carefully consider your strengths and aim to build a career around them.

If your path demands you to walk through hell, walk as if you own the place.

Striving is sexy, desire is sexy, transformation is sexy. Self-reliance, self-confidence, and self-discipline are sexy. Dependency is sexy, if it is chosen and not coercive. Symbiosis is sexy. Opposites are sexy.

Every accomplishment starts with the decision to try.

In every relationship, there is a 'reacher' and a 'settler'. Ideally both reach and settle for each other.

Do more things that make you forget to
check your phone.

If you find yourself in an abusive relationship, whether it's romantic or a friendship, have the courage to walk away. Life is too short to allow yourself to be mistreated or manipulated.

Boobs. They make suckers out of people.

Take care of your health. Protect your knees, avoid excessive sugary foods, and quit smoking as soon as possible.

If you can't look back at your younger self and realize that you were an idiot, you are probably still an idiot.

Your life is yours alone. Stand up and live it.

Turn off the news, turn on the music.

Love is spending the rest of your life with someone you want to kill and not doing it because you'd miss them.

Smoke-powder bombs are great against Cursed Skulls.

Try not to create pain or stress for others. You have no idea what other people have to carry on their shoulders.

Wrap it in latex or she'll get your paychecks.

Don't fall in love with the barkeeper or the barmaid.

Walk away from arguments that lead nowhere or, worse, to anger. Walk away from people who put you down. Walk away from the practice of pleasing people who choose to never see your worth. Walk away from any thought that undermines your peace of mind. Walk away from judgmental people. Walk away from your mistakes and fears; they do not determine your fate. The more you walk away from things that poison your soul, the healthier your life will be.

Only half of programming is coding. The other 90% is debugging.

Mistakes are painful when they happen, but years later, the collection of mistakes is called experience.

Strong women intimidate boys and excite men.

We live in an era in which companies pretend to care about social justice to sell products to people who pretend to hate capitalism.

You don't always need a plan; sometimes you just need guts.

Life is too short to not ask for what you want, in a relationship, in bed, in your career, or on your pizza.

You're only given one little spark of madness. You mustn't lose it.

Spending time with your wife is not optional. It is mandatory. Don't wait until you feel you should be with her; that is usually too late.

Only bet what you can afford to lose.

When someone criticizes you, always answer with 'Thank you for your feedback'.

You have got to take that next step, or you'll be doing the same shit for the rest of your life.

It's the little things that make life big.

If it's good, don't improve it; if it's bad, simplify it.

Learn to do a backflip.

Before you consider getting married and starting a family with someone, spend at least a couple of years together.

Rather be an honest asshole than a fucking liar.

Everyone has a chapter they don't read out loud.

Purpose is an incredible alarm clock.

Always be kind and understanding with your spouse.

Make a list of your tasks. Not a general to-do list; break it down into really small, manageable tasks. Do one task at a time.

Life is pointless. Live accordingly.

Small circle. Private life. Peaceful mind.

Be the person you need.

Brain cells die, skin cells die, hair cells die. But fat cells must have accepted Jesus Christ as their lord and savior because they seem to have eternal life.

Put a few sheets of toilet paper in the toilet before you go to avoid splashing.

Never half-ass two things. Whole-ass one thing.

The best argument against democracy is a five-minute conversation with the average voter.

Your value isn't diminished because of someone's inability to see your worth.

Do. Not. Procrastinate. Do it now.

If you are a parent or about to become one, know that your days seem long and stressful, but the years will seem to just pass very quickly. Treasure the time with your little ones.

Don't confuse a lesson for a soulmate.

Bananas contain high levels of potassium which makes them slightly radioactive. To minimize the risk of a harmful radiation dose you should never eat more than 600 bananas per second.

Humans gonna human. Don't ask why, don't try to argue; just keep the good ones in your life and the bad ones out.

Whenever you are feeling down, remember, you're the sperm that won.

Don't feel bad if your kid doesn't like you because you said no to something. Your job isn't to be liked all the time. Your job is to raise a decent, kind, and responsible human being.

Start to resist or cease to exist.

No one ever lay on their deathbed wishing they could have put more hours in at work.

Choose your battles wisely. You can't win every time. No one does. Besides, most battles do not change anything, so be smart.

Walk softly and carry a big gun.

If you touch them with your words first, your hands will go much further afterwards.

Don't seek happiness; create it.

The fact that so many successful politicians are such shameless liars, is not only a reflection on them, it is also a reflection on our society. When the people want the impossible, only liars can satisfy.

True freedom is when you can shit wherever you want.

A little nonsense now and then is relished by the best of men.

Respect your uniqueness and drop comparison. Relax into your being.

Family isn't always blood. It's the people in your life who want you in theirs. The ones who accept you for who you are. The ones who would do anything to see you smile and who love you no matter what.

Antidepressants don't cure poverty.

Have a relationship where you can sit around doing nothing, but still have fun because you're together.

If you fail to plan, you plan to fail.

Always check your brakes before driving.

Highway hypnosis is a mental state where a person can drive a vehicle great distances, responding to external events in the expected, safe, and correct manner with no recollection of having consciously done so.

Tomorrow is a new day and another chance to fuck things up just a little bit differently.

Attention is the rarest and purest form of generosity.

The only defense against evil, violent people is good people who are more skilled at violence.

Do a barrel roll. Come on.

Before peeling an orange, roll it around in your hand, squishing it ever so slightly, like you would a ball of play-dough, this will help separate the white sucky bits from the good bits.

Never slap someone who chews tobacco.

Touch some grass every once in a while.

You don't have to be the friend one hears from every day, but you should be the friend one can call on any day.

Be the extremist the media says you are.

Asking the government to fix the government is like asking cancer to cure cancer.

You do your thing and I do my thing. You are not in this world to live up to my expectations, and I am not in this world to live up to yours. You are you and I am I. And if by any chance we find each other, it's beautiful. If not, it can't be helped.

Blind belief in authority is the greatest enemy of truth.

Be romantic, but be dirty.

If violent crime is to be curbed, it is only the intended victim who can do it. The felons do not fear the police. They fear neither judge nor jury. Therefore, what they must be taught to fear is their victims.

In the evening and at night, your thoughts are more negative than during daytime because your body wants you to sleep. So don't deep-think at night, count your blessings to free your mind.

Be peace, love, and light. And a little 'go fuck yourself'.

Words have consequences; silence too.

You are never too old to throw random shit into other people's shopping carts while they aren't looking.

To be ignorant of the past is to be forever a child.

If you see any mistake made by others in writing, just ignroe it.

The only failure is not to try.

If you catch 100 red fire ants and 100 large black ants and put them in a jar, nothing will happen at first. However, if you violently shake the jar, and dump them back on the ground, the ants will fight until they eventually kill each other. The red ants think the black ants are the enemy and vice versa, when in reality, the real enemy is the person who shook the jar. This is exactly what is happening in society today, and the question we should be asking ourselves is who's shaking the jar and why?

The harder the life, the stronger you will become. The stronger you become, the easier the life will get.

A world without freedom of speech is a world of slavery and tyranny.

'I'm just gonna get gas in the morning.' is among the worst decisions you can make as an adult.

You make your life hard by always being in your head. Life is simple; get out of your head and get into the moment.

Hyenas have sex six times a day. That's why they are always laughing and happy.

Decide that you want it more than you are afraid of it.

You are free to choose, but you are not free from the consequence of your choice.

If it's out of your hands, it deserves freedom from your mind too.

The difference between a politician and a flying pig is the letter F.

Stop comparing yourself to others. Flowers are pretty, but so are sunsets, and they look nothing alike.

Fear is a reaction. Courage is a decision.

Never let your girlfriend and your wife meet each other.

Talk less and listen more. This way, you will know what you know as well as what others know, without them knowing what you know.

Learn what a 'Single Discretionary Allowance' is.

Close your eyes and dance.

Your beliefs don't make you a better person; your behavior does.

Travel as much as you can.

You never realize how strong you are until being strong is the only choice you have.

Sexy is an energy, not a body type.

Give a man a fish, and he'll eat for a day. Teach a man to fish, and you can bang his wife for the entire weekend.

Work out because you love your body, not because you hate it.

Write a diary. Just a few lines on what you did during the day. The days will stop rushing by as quickly.

Sacrificing comfort, and suffering the dullness of studying, is suffering you remove from your future life.

It's never the future that you are afraid of. It's repeating the past that makes you anxious.

True love is when both people think that they are the lucky one.

Listen, smile, agree, and then do whatever the fuck you were gonna do anyway.

Life is too short to tolerate shit that doesn't make you happy.

How to have a beach body: have a body, go to the beach.

Physical attraction is beautiful, but it's the intimate mental attraction that is rare, highly intoxicating, and powerfully addictive.

Stretch and forgive.

Dogs never lie about love.

The quieter you become, the more you can hear.

Unexpected friendships are the best ones.

Character is how you treat those who can do nothing for you.

You either understand history or you trust the government. You can't do both.

Sometimes you have to let go of what you thought your life would be like and find joy in the story you are actually living.

Gambling-games are designed to make you lose money. Don't be a loser, don't gamble.

Love yourself. You need self-love to be able to be loved by others. Know you deserve the best and fight for that.

Don't quit. Sometimes the things you are hoping for come at unexpected times.

The goal is to die with memories, not dreams.

A lot of people seem normal until you get to know them.

All the animals outside are free. If you catch them, you can keep them.

Sometimes people who are really far away from you can make you feel better than the people right beside you.

Never miss an opportunity to use the bathroom, even if you don't have to go that bad, and especially on long mini-bus rides in Thailand.

A good life is when you smile often, dream big, laugh a lot, and realize how blessed you are with what you have.

You can dilute dish soap 20 to 1 and put it in a spray bottle. It lasts much longer, and you get the same results. You can do the same with shampoo and conditioner. Waste less, pay less.

Worrying won't stop the bad stuff from happening. It just stops you from enjoying the good.

When you buy a used car, look at the tires. If the tires are in a good condition and of a well known brand, the rest of the car is most likely in a good condition as well. If the tires are cheap and worn down, find another car. If the previous owners could afford good tires, the rest of the car is most likely well looked after as well.

If you have a clear shot and a good shovel, there is no need to call the police.

Some things don't work out because you deserve better.

If printing money would end poverty, printing diplomas would end stupidity.

To check if something's electrified, put the back of your hand to it. DC (direct current) will have you clench your fist. AC (alternating current), well, it'll give you a face-slap-reminder to turn things off first.

Always remember the KISS rule: Keep it simple, stupid.

Despondency is our biggest enemy.

That stupid walk you do when someone is mopping a floor, and you know you are going to walk over it, but you want them to see how sorry you are, so you make yourself look like you are walking over hot coals.

If they let their friends insult you or talk down to you, dump them. They won't stand up for you when it really matters either.

Express your love to your parents and grandparents. They badly need it. Especially your Dad.

Social media is like having nosy neighbors who don't really like you. Most people just stay connected to look over the fence and see what you are doing.

This is one for the ladies: 'mansplaining' is short for 'man explaining'.

Your alarm sound is basically your theme song, since its plays at the start of every episode.

A smart pilot doesn't eject in a tunnel.

Do not use a battering ram when an arrow will do.

The art of life lies in a constant readjustment to our surroundings.

The trouble with most trouble is that it starts out as fun.

Long ago, exactly one cat died from being fed four minutes past feeding time. Cats have told their children this story for thousands of generations.

In the end, our choices make us.

If you meet somebody and you heart pounds, your hands shake, and your knees go weak, that's not the one. When you meet your soulmate, you will feel calm. No anxiety, no agitation.

Cook bacon in the oven, not in a pan.

Don't get into debt unless you have at least 25% of what you think you'll need.

Find someone with whom you can lay in bed all day and trade sexual favors for trips to the fridge.

Always tell your spouse you love them. Whoever said never to go to bed angry, never had to get up at 2am to go to work. The key is to not let yesterday's arguments affect your today.

The art of life lies in a constant readjustment to our surroundings.

Buy yourself a rice cooker. It will change your life.

Perfection is a goal that must forever be striven for but never achieved. Do your best to keep improving, but don't ever let your ego tell you that you've learned enough. You can never have enough knowledge.

Whether you think you can, or you think you can't, you'll be right in both cases.

If you ever get arrested, before you say anything, demand to have an attorney present or ask for a duty solicitor.

Feeling sad and depressed? Are you anxious and worried about the future? Do you feel isolated and alone? You might suffer from capitalism.

If you have to bury a body, put an animal carcass on top of it. It will fool any police dog.

The more you expect things to be a certain way, the more disappointed you'll be. Accept life as it is and you'll be free.

It's no bad thing to celebrate a simple life.

It is very important to love someone a little extra on their bad days.

Get a passive income as soon as possible. Money you don't have to work for is always nice, and easy to save.

Never iron your clothes naked.

Magic Johnson wasted the world's best porn star name on a basketball career.

RSVP'ing 'maybe next time' to a wedding invite isn't the correct response.

At some point, each person in your life will experience their final day with you.

In heated moments, always think before you speak.

Cycling is bad for the economy. A cyclist doesn't buy a car, and does not take out a car loan, does not buy car insurance, and does not buy fuel. He does not send his car for servicing and repairs, does not use paid parking, and does, most likely, not become obese. Healthy people are not needed for the economy. They do not buy drugs. They do not go to hospitals or doctors. They add nothing to a country's GDP.

Race only matters to racists. The rest cares about character.

Last chances don't come with warnings.

If you mark text and press 'Command + Shift + T' on a Mac, it will read it to you.

Don't buy the cheapest trash bags.

Life will knock you down a few times. It will show you things you'd never want to see. You will experience sadness and failures. But you will get through it, you will always get back up.

Art is making a thing and then trying to make a better one, and then continuing to do this until you die.

Your thoughts are not your own; they are the product of your environment.

We live by trial and error. Mostly error. A shit ton of error.

Love your enemy, but keep your gun oiled.

Be your own muse.

If there is an oil crisis, and oil companies are making record profits, a healthcare crisis, and healthcare companies are making record profits, a financial crisis, and finance companies are making record profits, then the companies are the problem.

Sniff glue and worship Satan.

The greatest wealth is to live content with little.

The moment you choose not to allow events or people to control your emotions, inner peace begins.

Step over ants, put worms back in the grass, rescue baby caterpillars, release spiders back into your garden, open windows for bees so they can fly home. All little souls deserve life too. Except mosquitos. Those fuckers got to die.

Find someone who is only crazy enough to make the sex good.

Wise people speak because they have something to say; fools because they have to say something.

No replay. No rewind. Enjoy every moment.

Never stop being a good person because of bad people.

Rest, nature, books, music. Such is the idea of happiness.

A problem shared is still a problem. So keep your issues to yourself.

Focus on one thing at a time and control your mind. Your mind is a monkey that needs to be controlled.

Life is an echo. What you send out, comes back. What you sow, you reap. What you give, you get. What you see in others, exists in you.

It's better to walk alone, than with a crowd going in the wrong direction.

Often the only difference between a good and a bad day is your attitude.

Where there is preparation, there is no fear.

Cherish the possibility of having a dream come true. It's what makes life interesting.

Learning never exhausts the mind.

Sometimes the best revenge is to smile and move on.

You can take most meds even a decade after they expired. Except insulin, nitroglycerin, and liquid antibiotics.

Don't spend money you don't have.

There are 1500 newspapers, 1100 magazines, 9000 radio stations, 1500 TV stations, and 2400 publishers, owned by only 6 corporations.

Sometimes it is beautiful to stay silent when someone expects you to be enraged.

Rumors are started by haters, carried by fools, and accepted by idiots.

Relationships don't last because of the good times; they last because the hard times were handled with love and care.

If you can't remember things, write them down.

It's a man's job to respect a woman, but it's a woman's job to give him something to respect.

You are not special. So chill out.

If you hate everything and everyone, eat something. If you feel like everyone hates you, sleep. If you feel like you hate yourself, work out and have a hot shower.

The price of anything is the amount of life you exchange for it.

To hell with circumstances. Create opportunities.

You alone are enough. You have nothing to prove to anybody.

Nipples. Without them, tits would be pointless.

Drinking water on an empty stomach purifies the colon, making it easier to absorb nutrients. Drinking water in the morning increases the production of new blood, and muscle cells. Drinking chilled water can boost your metabolism. Water helps to purge toxins from the blood which helps to keep your skin glowing and clear. And water balances your lymph system, helping your body to fight infections. Drink lots of water.

Listen to your gut feeling. It's your life's compass.

Kindness begins with understanding that we all struggle.

Don't vomit against the wind, especially not from a moving car.

A gentleman is one who puts more into the world than he takes out.

Before was was was, was was is.

If your temper rises, withdraw your hand. If your hand rises, withdraw your temper.

Don't work the night shift. It may seem a good choice, but you will not see or speak to people you love for days.

Don't let a bunch of greedy selfish fools ruin our whole planet.

Rule your mind, or your mind will rule you.

Don't try and convince the people closest to you of your views, if they disagree with you. Relationships keep you grounded and connected. Don't risk meaningful connections for the brief satisfaction you'd get from winning an argument.

It's a good practice not to cover the entire bill on a first date. If there's a genuine connection, you can share the expenses.

Be curious, not judgmental.

To act without clear understanding, to form habits without investigation, to follow a path all one's life without knowing where it leads; such is the behavior of the multitude.

Pick your battles and cut your losses.

Don't put salsa on all of your tacos at the same time, only on the one you are about to eat. That way they won't get soggy.

Learn the basics of Power Query in Excel. You'll save a ton of time when it comes to repetitive tasks.

All you need is a clear vision and a burning desire.

Think. It's not illegal yet.

Life's decision-making isn't a multiple-choice test with a clear 'right' answer. You picked choice A, and oops, the outcome was a disaster. But who's to say option B wouldn't have been a bigger mess? Don't chase 'being right'. Focus on making informed choices. Good decisions come from doing your homework, gathering intel, and then taking the plunge. And remember: action beats overthinking any day.

You are the universe expressing itself as a human for a while.

A salary is the drug they give you to forget your dreams.

Dishwasher tabs are also very effective for cleaning toilets. Put one into the toilet's tank and let it dissolve. Next time you flush, you will clean your toilet automatically.

You need truth. You need stillness. You don't need more sleep; you need to wake up and live.

All people are the same; only their habits differ.

Moments become memories, and people become lessons. That's life.

To remove a tick, strike a match, blow it out, and hold the still hot match to the tick's body. It will think there is a forest fire and let go after a couple of seconds. You can then simply pull it out.

You should pull on every door. If it is a pull door, it will open. If it is a push door, you will pull yourself toward the door and the momentum will open the door for you.

He who is unable to live in society, must be either a beast or a god.

Find a way to monetize your craft. Selling your hours to a company is a terrible way to make money.

Read more books and never cease your quest for knowledge.

The most advanced thing you can do is the basics, consistently.

You don't need more sleep. It's your soul that is tired, not your body. You need nature, you need magic. You need adventure, and freedom.

You can use vinegar to neutralize tear gas.

When you have been towing a load or driving fast with your car, don't turn the engine off immediately after you stop. Leave it on idle for a minute so it can gradually cool off instead of instantly. That way your engine will last much longer. This is especially true for cars with turbos.

If you ever sense that you're on the verge of a mental breakdown, take a step back, assess the root cause of the problem, and if you can't resolve it, try removing it from your life altogether.

Forgive yourself and keep moving forward.

When people ask you what you do for a living, they calculate the level of respect to give you.

Make sure the juice is worth the squeeze.

When writing, proper punctuation greatly reduces confusion and allows the reader to better comprehend what you are attempting to convey.

When it comes to drugs, remember: you can't miss what you don't know.

If you put freshly cooked potatoes in ice water, they become very easy to peel.

If you have a moped or motorbike, get yourself a 'Goldplug'. It's a special oil sump bolt. It has a neodymium magnet on its tip and helps the oil filter by catching metal shards in the oil.

It's recommended to drink about 30 ml of water per 1 kg bodyweight, per day. About 1oz per 2 lbs.

The greatest takeaway from Buddhism is to always go for the middle ground in literally everything in life.

Don't marry the first person who gives you an orgasm.

The only way to forget the mistakes you made in the past is to make even bigger and graver mistakes in the present.

Living in moderation is beneficial for your mental and physical health. (Social) media and the internet made us forget that.

Visit your parents while you still can.

Every decision is binary.

You cannot protect yourself from sadness without protecting yourself from happiness.

Have faith in yourself and trust your potential. Be fearless. Be confident. Be happy.

There will always be better, and there will always be worse. Be grateful for who you are and what you have.

When you brush with a broom, brush towards yourself so you collect the dirt instead of brushing it away from you and dispersing it.

Never get so busy making a living that you forget to make a life.

Do something you are afraid of every now and then. Expand your comfort zone.

Don't let people who do little for you, control your mind, feelings, and emotions.

Always mind Murphy's laws. Everything that can go wrong will go wrong.

Eating too much cake is gluttony; it's a sin. However, eating too much pie is okay because the sin of pi is always zero.

Time does not change everything. Doing things changes things. Not doing things leaves things exactly as they were.

Do not make the same mistake twice.

If a service is free, you are not the customer. You are the product.

The only place where success comes before work is in the dictionary.

Learn when to say no. It solves a lot of problems.

The more you research, the crazier you sound to ignorant people.

Respect yourself enough to walk away from anything that no longer serves you, grows you, or makes you happy.

When you start training, it takes about 4 weeks for you to see any changes to your body, about 8 weeks for your friends and family, and about 12 weeks for the rest of the world. Keep going.

Put two ice cubes in hot ramen to cool it down enough to not burn your tongue.

Most of the jobs, that you usually call a repairman for, can be done with basic knowledge, cheap tools, and 5-minute short YouTube videos. Changing electric sockets or laying tiles is much simpler than you think.

Not everyone who is confident is competent, and not everyone, who is competent is confident.

Your mind is everything. What you think, you become. Mental health and a purpose should be your number one priority.

Do some form of daily self-care and self-improvement, even if it's just a little bit of stretching.

If you have sunburns, apply yogurt to the burned area. It will cool your skin and help it heal.

It didn't start with gas chambers. It started with one party controlling the media. One party controlling the message. One party deciding what the truth is. One party censoring speech and silencing opposition. One party dividing citizens into 'us' and 'them'. It started when good people turned a blind eye and let it happen.

Be nice to people who have access to your toothbrush.

Don't use earbuds for too long; they will screw up your hearing.

How to stop time: kiss. How to travel in time: read. How to escape time: music. How to feel time: write. How to release time: breathe.

'Windows key + D' will minimize all windows and show the desktop.

Never fart while wearing noise-canceling headphones.

If you want to go fast, go alone. If you want to go far, go together.

Don't save something for a special occasion; every day of your life is a special occasion. Champagne expires after 2-3 years.

If you can make a girl laugh, you can make her do anything.

If you are reading this, you've been in a coma for almost 20 years. We are trying a new technique. We don't know where this message will end up in your dream, but we hope we are getting through. Please wake up.

Nothing on earth is more luxurious than a comfortable sofa, a good book, and a nice hot beverage.

For your own sanity, let things be.

Deescalate aggressive behavior or insults by saying that you understand and that you kind of agree.

The rich and powerful piss on us, and the media tells us it is raining.

If you want to lower your stress level, breathing is everything. Take a deep breath, hold, and follow up with an additional deep breath. Then slowly exhale.

Appear weak when you are strong, and strong when you are weak.

No one rules if no one obeys.

When your grandparents share their life stories with you during your younger years, take the time to listen and consider documenting their experiences. It may not seem particularly captivating at the time, but you'll come to appreciate having preserved their memories as you grow older.

Stop waiting for life to be easy. Stop hoping for somebody to save you. Face some hard facts and you can have an incredible life.

Learn how to lucid dream and unlock your hidden potentials.

If you find yourself torn between two choices, flip a coin. As the coin is in the air, notice which side you secretly hope it will land on. That's your answer.

Give a man a fish and you will feed him for a day. Give a man a pair of concrete shoes and neither he nor the fishes will ever be hungry again.

Try being informed instead of just opinionated.

Emotions neither prove nor disprove facts. There was a time when any rational adult understood this. But years of dumbed-down education and emphasis on how people 'feel' have left too many people unable to see through this media gimmick.

Never fight an old man. If you win, you beat up an old man. If you lose, you got beaten up by an old man.

Learn how to take notes. Read books to extend your attention span. Learn how to use the internet properly. Learn as much as you can.

Enjoy the little things. We are living in such a fast-paced society that we often overlook those happy moments. Even when you're busy achieving your goals, treat yourself and have some fun once in a while.

Unlimited tolerance must lead to the disappearance of tolerance. If we extend unlimited tolerance even to those who are intolerant, if we are not prepared to defend a tolerant society against the onslaught of the intolerant, then the tolerant will be destroyed, and tolerance with them.

If you are dealing with a mild illness like a simple cough, it's advisable to steer clear of carbohydrates as they can potentially promote bacterial growth. Eat green vegetables, fats, and proteins. Ensure you stay well-hydrated by consuming about four liters of liquids per day, including vegetable juices and herbal teas.

Don't keep toxic people anywhere near your life, even if they are family.

If you don't respect a person, it should be impossible for them to insult you. If they don't deserve your respect, their opinions don't matter. If someone you respect insults you, either take it into consideration or reevaluate your opinion of them.

Kindness is not an act. It is a lifestyle.

Never argue with idiots; they'll drag you down to their level and beat you with experience.

Wanting always interrupts being.

Keep your nails trimmed and clean.

That awkward moment between birth and death.

Real eyes realize real lies.

Only spend money on things that you really value. Don't be a marketing victim.

Never date someone who doesn't respect your spouse.

If you dream you are a chicken, don't lay eggs.

If you ever think 'the government would never do that', look up 'Operation Mockingbird', 'MKUltra', 'Tuskegee Experiment', 'MKNAOMI', or 'Operation Northwoods'.

Brush your teeth like your life depends on it. Because it does.

Go to the toilet before your morning shower, and always plunge a toilet with your mouth closed.

When a cop pulls you over in the United States of America, put both of your hands on top of the steering wheel.

An 'I don't give a fuck about people's opinions' attitude is great, but be careful not to end up as the most hated person around.

The reasonable man adapts himself to the world. The unreasonable one persists in trying to adapt the world to himself. Therefore, all progress depends on the unreasonable man.

When you get angry, take a breath and count to 10. Throw a punch at 8. Nobody expects that.

Keep your nose hair trimmed and clean.

There is no blinker fluid.

You don't always have to agree, but try to respect and understand other opinions.

Don't sweat the petty stuff, and don't pet the sweaty stuff.

Cats have 32 muscles in each ear to help them ignore you.

Life is short; make sure you spend a lot of time arguing online with strangers.

Stalin once ripped all the feathers off a live chicken as a lesson to his followers. He set the chicken on the floor. The chicken was bloodied and suffering immensely, yet, when Stalin began to toss some bits of wheat toward the chicken, it followed him around. He said to his followers, "This is how easy it is to govern stupid people. They will follow you no matter how much pain you cause them, as long as you throw them a little worthless treat once in a while."

Haters gonna hate, and ain'ters gonna ain't.

Your beliefs don't make you a better person. Your behavior does.

Nature is the new nightclub.

Don't shave your privates before going on a hiking trip.

The thoughts you think and the way you feel are at the center of what you attract.

Don't date coworkers or classmates.

Almost everything can wait until tomorrow. Prioritize your own well-being, tasks, and desires over your boss's or your company's work, unless a situation is genuinely critical, with potential catastrophic consequences. Don't compromise your happiness, or mental health for the sake of someone else's agenda.

Make it look easy if you have to work hard.

Never completely close doors in your life. Whether it's with a former partner or a challenging boss, if you part on good terms, you leave without creating animosity and with the potential to ask for a favor in the future.

The European Consumer Centres Network (ECC Net) offers legal assistance if your products break in the EU and you need them replaced or repaired, while still under warranty, of course.

A wise man once told his wife nothing.

In life, you will have to choose between suffering and boredom.

If you have a high temperature, you can try to bring it down with vinegar. Soak a rag in apple vinegar and place it on your forehead for an hour. You can also put vinegar socks on your feet. Squeeze them out so they are not dripping wet.

Never sign a contract straight away. Consider every offer carefully, be it mobile contracts, work contracts, or loans. Think about any big decision like the next decade of your life depends on it, because often enough it does.

Whenever you buy cosmetics, don't take the first ones on the shelf. Customers often open them to check the color, fragrance, etc.

Decide to be happy.

Sometimes the light at the end of the tunnel is a train.

Never argue with drunk people.

A lot of love is lost between what is said and not meant, and what is meant and not said.

Sooner or later, you will find that physical attraction is no longer enough, and you'll long for real human connection, real passion.

In a society that profits from your self-doubt, liking yourself is a rebellious act.

When older people say 'enjoy them while they are young', they are talking about your knees and hips, not your kids.

Maintaining respectful boundaries in relationships, especially with friends and their spouses, is essential to avoid potential complications and misunderstandings.

Don't expect to get if you don't ask.

Never make important decisions late at night. Sleep on it.

Keep being curious and keep learning. You're never too old to try out something new.

Coke can help unclog your toilet if you don't have anything else, because it is mildly acidic. Just pour in about two lines and leave it for a couple of hours before you flush.

Fake it till you make it.

Have a completely packed toiletry bag with your own essentials in your wardrobe. It saves you time packing, especially when it comes to spontaneous trips. An extra USB cable for your electronic devices is also a good idea.

If it doesn't bring you energy, inspiration or orgasms, it doesn't belong in your life.

Live in the past, moment, and future. Learn from the past, enjoy the moment, and plan for the future.

Apply for a higher-paying job at least every two years.

Testing your nerves and patience constantly won't make them stronger. It will leave scars and make them weaker.

If you want great advice, just ask yourself, what would Uncle Iroh do.

Never give 100% at a new job.

Feel free to say no to the things that you do not want without having to explain yourself.

Muscle grows when it recovers from damage done by training, not by the training itself.

Too little perfume is better than too much.

Journaling helps to clear the mind of life's bullshit.

Be punctual.

Wednesday is like the middle finger of the week.

Life is absurd.

Doing something just a little bit gradually will still get you infinitely farther than doing nothing.

It's never too late to get braces.

Don't confuse the truth with the opinion of the majority.

Social skills are like any other skill. The better you are at it, the more fun you'll have.

Have three hobbies. One for your body. One for your mind. And one to make money.

For the perfect running form, look ahead with your eyes and keep your head up. Keep your jaw relaxed and your mouth slightly open. Hold yourself upright and don't bend at the waist; lean forward at your ankles instead. Consciously drop and relax your shoulders.

The little things, the little moments — they aren't little.

Treat others the way you want to be treated.

Insert commas into your passwords so when your credentials are hacked and dumped into a CSV, it breaks it.

Make friends with people who celebrate when you succeed, and avoid the people who put you down when you speak of your accomplishments.

If you wait until you are ready, you'll be waiting for the rest of your life.

Let whoever think whatever.

Fart when people hug you. It makes them feel strong.

Sex is nobody's business except the three people involved.

The best portion of your life will be the small, nameless moments you spend smiling with someone who matters to you.

Don't stress about the dumb shit.

An emotionally unavailable person will make you feel like your basic needs are too much.

If you don't want to clean your gas stove every time you cook, put aluminum foil on it and cut out the gas pit areas. When it becomes too dirty, simply replace the foil.

No matter what you are going through, always try to help people. So instead of saying 'Fuck off' ask, 'How can I help you to fuck off?'.

Intelligence and a dirty mind are a fantastic combination.

You don't know what people think. Most likely they're not passing judgment or harboring negative feelings about you; in fact, they typically just don't care. People tend to forget the things you've said or done. Be direct and don't expect others to know what you're thinking if you haven't expressed your thoughts.

Eat lots of fruit, hydrate, do your squats, and stay away from negativity.

Fighting doesn't solve problems. But if you can't avoid a fight, throw the first punch.

A balanced diet is having a cupcake in each hand.

You did not wake up today to be a weak-ass bitch.

Remember when everyone knew World Wrestling Entertainment was fake, and the fans didn't care and continued to watch anyway? We are almost there with politics and media.

When you are consumed by thoughts, write. When you are uninspired, read.

You can never laugh too much or have too many orgasms.

Life is meaningless, but you can use that to your advantage. Nothing you do is wrong, regardless of what you are doing. If you feel that something is right for you, it is. There is no greater meaning to anything. If people laugh at you, you are the only one assigning the label that being laughed at is bad. This concept can be applied to almost anything in life.

There's only one thing more precious than our time, and that's who we spend it on.

Find a healthy balance between doing your best and not giving a fuck.

Clouds probably sometimes look down on us and say "This one is shaped like an idiot".

Every machine is a smoke machine if you operate it wrong enough.

Good steaks are like good men. The best ones have a little fat on them.

Have a budget routine and make your family, your spouse and children, a priority. Have an emergency reserve, but don't forget to set something aside for fun and silly things you may fancy.

If you ever have a grease clog in your sink, pour a whole bottle of liquid soap into it and flush with some HOT water. Wait for 30 minutes and flush again with more hot water. Chances are you saved yourself a plumber. Also, oil and grease don't go in the sink. Use paper towels to clean that stuff out of your pans before you wash them.

The decline of civilization can be traced back to when they stopped putting toys in cereal boxes.

Keep going. Keep going. Keep going. Keep going. Keep going. Keep going.

You can admire someone's beauty without questioning your own.

Happiness is not an endless pursuit; it is what you choose.

The healer also needs healing. The planner also needs surprises. The giver also needs to receive. The thoughtful also needs to be thought of. The considerate also needs to be considered.

Don't pick your friends just because they are fun to get drunk with.

Don't stay in an abusive relationship. You deserve to be loved, cared for, and respected, but you need to believe that for it to work.

Once weapons were manufactured to fight wars. Now wars are manufactured to sell weapons.

Never apologize for the fire in you.

One day you will wake up in this place, where everything feels right. Your heart will be calm, your soul will be lit. Your thoughts will be positive and your vision clear. You'll be at peace with where you've been and at peace with what you have been through.

There are strong, independent women who still want their hands held and foreheads kissed.

One way to get out of a conversation is to take off one of your socks and hand it to the person talking.

Alternate buying brown and white eggs so you'll always know which ones are old.

Grinding glass to a powder and mixing it with cocaine will make your customers get their kick more easily, while simultaneously making them more tolerant due to mucous scarring. This, in turn, will make them overdose more frequently, ensuring a healthy customer rotation and reducing the junkies in your customer base.

Never stop doing what you like because of a relationship.

The wonderful thing about true laughter is that is just destroys any kind of system of dividing people.

You. Are. Doing. Great.

Everything will fade into mist; the past will be erased, and the erasure will be forgotten.

Always follow the money; it will show you the truth behind any conspiracy.

If someone close to you asks you to stop drinking, stop drinking.

You are exactly where you need to be because if you were supposed to be somewhere else, you would be there.

Never play leapfrog with a unicorn.

If she says she is crazy, believe her and run.

Your parents and teachers have no idea what they are doing, so take their advice with a grain of salt. Their experience might not apply to your life. Things change.

Silence rides shotgun wherever hate goes. There is no such thing as an innocent bystander.

If the tip of an avocado becomes black, it is spoiled.

17.4 kHz is known as 'the mosquito' frequency. It can cause hearing damage, trigger seizures, and can create problems for animals.

You have a superpower, and it's called empathy.

If you want to push your kid toward a decision, don't ask yes or no questions but questions like "do you wanna brush your teeth with the blue or green toothbrush?"

When your dog is over 10 years old, you should screen for cancer once a year.

It's okay if it takes a little longer than you thought.

Who you are becoming is more important than who you've been.

Call your mom while you still can.

If we've been bamboozled long enough, we tend to reject any evidence of the bamboozle. We are no longer interested in finding out the truth. The bamboozle has captured us. It is simply too painful to acknowledge, even to ourselves, that we've been taken. Once you give a charlatan power over you, you almost never get it back.

Too many humans, not enough souls.

No risk, no story.

Get the fuck up and enjoy this life.

Satan loves you for who you are.

Always clean windows and mirrors from top to bottom.

When purchasing a second-hand car, put cardboard under the engine and turn the car on. Then talk with the owner for at least five minutes. Check to see if there is any fluid on the cardboard. After this, take the car for a 10-minute test drive, park it up, leave the engine running, and put the cardboard under. Again, wait five minutes before checking. This will save you a lot of headaches and money.

No war but class war.

We judge others by what they do, but ourselves by our intentions.

Consider checking your testosterone level if you are aged 35 or older. A healthy testosterone level make all the difference as it is related to muscles, fat loss, mood, energy, and appearance.

Nobody dies a virgin. Life fucks us all.

Breathe in, breathe out. Whatever happens in life, happens. Take things as they are and move on.

Be valuable, not available.

The only essential oil a man needs is WD-40.

It is only illegal if you get caught.

There is a past version of you that is proud of how far you have come.

See a therapist even if you don't think you need one. It will save you a world of trouble. Making decisions with an unhealthy mind can cost you big-time.

Dry coffee grounds can be used as nourishment for your plants.

Always go to the bathroom with your kids before a road trip.

Other people's lack of planning does not constitute an emergency on your part.

Sometimes we are homesick for a place we are not sure even exists.

The closer you get to nature, the further you are from idiots.

Religion is like a penis. It's okay to have one and it's ok to be proud of it. However, do not pull it out in public, do not push it on to children, do not write laws with it. And don't think with it.

Write more love letters.

Cooking on high heat seals the flavors in food like steaks and stir-fried vegetables. Cooking on low heat releases the flavors into soups, stock, or sauces.

Women are bad at parking only because they are constantly lied to about what eight inches, or 20 centimeters, are.

Sex and art are the same thing.

You can save the pins of your credit cards and debit cards as contacts in your phone. Paging Doctor Spend-Some.

Start your day by drinking half a liter of water (roughly a US pint). The body dehydrates during sleep, primarily through breathing. Replenish that, and you'll have a totally different energy level in the morning.

If you are good all the time, you will turn into a dessert and they will eat you.

Hard work doesn't feel like hard work when you are doing what you love.

Who knows why we were taught to fear the witches, and not those who burned them alive.

Half a cup of salt will dehydrate and kill you in matter of hours.

If you start every phone call with 'my battery is about to die', you can hang up on them whenever you want.

Eat less meat.

Clutter smothers. Simplicity breathes.

You can use a T-shirt as a pillowcase.

Read banned books.

Learn to cook and eat well for the rest of your life.

Fold your worries into paper planes and turn them into flying fucks.

Avoid physical confrontation at all costs. But if you ever have to fight, fight like you're the third monkey trying to make it onto Noah's Ark.

Enjoy what you enjoy with pride.

Never be ashamed; nobody is perfect.

Comfy clothes, good food, peace and quiet.

Always assume you're a moron, so you'll hold yourself back and not embarrass yourself or make a situation worse.

Be kind and smile; it's infectious.

A small compliment can make someones day.

Free your inner child, but be careful, it might be a mean little shit.

If it's not yours, don't take it. If it's not right, don't do it. If it's not true, don't say it. And if you don't know, shut up.

Great sex can do the work of a thousand psychiatrists.

Find a valve for your emotions. Talk to people, write, make art.

Care for yourself before you care for others.

Self-reflect and better yourself. It's never too late to live a fulfilled life.

Find out what you truly want and work towards it.

It's not your fault that the world is stupid.

Enjoy as much art as you can.

Changing the battery in your car keys is much easier than you think.

You can't drink all day if you don't start early.

Locksmiths often abuse an emergency situation. Only pay if you get an official invoice, and if it's too high, contact consumer protection services and take legal action.

To extend the battery life of your phone, try to keep its charge above 85%.

When your girl complains about things, don't offer solutions. Just listen and show empathy.

Expect the expected.

Drink some water, you beautiful and capable but dehydrated bitch.

The real secret to a fabulous life is to live imperfectly with great delight.

Keep the instruction manuals of the stuff you buy. Put them in a binder and keep the sacred texts. You never know when you might need them.

'Twunt'. Because sometimes 'twat' or 'cunt' just aren't enough.

Gratitude is the mother of all virtue.

If you hear weird noises in the night, simply make weirder noises to assert dominance.

You're too poor to buy cheap shoes. Buy quality stuff that will last and save you money in the long run.

If your flight is delayed, don't be mean or angry with the people behind the counter, they will do as much as they can, and if you're an asshole, they will stick you with the worst options possible.

Unclench your jaw and loosen up your shoulders, you stressed hunchback.

Doing stuff to keep yourself busy while avoiding what really needs to be done is called productive procrastination.

Being single means using the other half of your bed for remotes, pillows, snacks, laptop, and phone.

When you focus on problems you will have more problems. When you focus on possibilities, you will have more opportunities.

Don't bite the hand that fingered you, or whatever people say.

Once you know the freedom of letting go, you'll regret that you ever held on.

It's time to get up and get going. Today's bad decisions aren't going to make themselves.

Making new friends as an adult is hard because the people you would get along with best also don't want to leave their house.

Focus on improving yourself, not proving yourself.

Clean as you go. A few minutes of cleaning each day will help you stay on top of the clutter and dirt, and will prevent you from getting overwhelmed. One day you can clean the bathroom. Next day, do a little bit of vacuuming. Another day, a bit of dusting. A lot can be done in ten minutes.

You can get cannabis resin off your fingers with any type of cooking oil. Wash with soap and water afterwards.

Karma is only a bitch if you are.

Denture cleaning tablets are great for cleaning bottles.

Breaking news is breaking you.

It is possible to find both love and friendship in one person.

Moving to a different country rarely is the best decision, but you will not see many people confess to that.

We are all the devil in someone's story.

Only fake flowers are flawless.

They say it's easier to open bananas at the lower end.

Never stop pushing yourself. Some say 8 hours of sleep is enough. Why stop there? Why not 9? Why not 10? Strive for greatness.

Guess why Peter Pan didn't want to grow up.

The average person thinks they are above average.

Enjoy your life today. Yesterday is gone; tomorrow might never come.

People do not decide their future. They decide to pick up habits and their habits decide their future.

Always smell it first.

Put on your coat before you answer your front door. If it's someone you don't want to see, you can always tell them that you are on your way out. If it is someone you do want to see, you can simply say that you just arrived at home.

Having a corpse in the car doesn't mean you can use the carpool lane.

At the end of the day, you'd rather be excluded for who you include than be included for who you exclude.

There are no guilty pleasures. If you like something, do it.

The harder you work for something, the greater you'll feel when you achieve it.

Don't pee on elevator buttons.

If you haven't grown up by the age of 50, you don't have to grow up at all.

Two things define us: Our patience when we have nothing and our attitude when we have everything.

If you find yourself in a fair fight, your tactics suck.

Most problems aren't solved with more thinking; they are solved with less thinking and more doing.

Work hard when you are at work. Play hard in your free time. And keep the two separate from each other.

Dismount a motorcycle only when stationary.

It's important to get out of the house every once in a while to remind yourself why you usually don't go out.

What is meant for you will always feel natural, calm and clear, not forced, chaotic and confused.

Talking about our problems is our greatest addiction. Break the habit. Talk about your joys.

If you pay attention to the patterns of your life, you'll realize that everything works out in the end. Everything takes you to a greater destination. You always grow, and the things you think you can't survive, you somehow always make it through.

Worrying does not take away tomorrow's troubles. It takes away todays peace.

Treat others with compassion and patience, but never allow yourself to be surprised by bad people or taken advantage of.

Don't chase butterflies.
Fix your garden, and the butterflies
will come.

Sometimes you will not know the value of a moment until it becomes a memory.

Exercise four times a week. Learn how to defend yourself. Read books. Have a hobby. Learn a second language. Keep a months worth of food and water at home for emergencies. Have a good first aid kit and a fire extinguisher at home, and install carbon monoxide detectors throughout your place.

Be a warrior not a worrier.

You don't need to hop on every trend. Trends come and go every year. Focus on work you care about. Don't give into the fear of missing out.

Do not put chili peppers in the microwave for too long.

Plan something. It's important to have something to look forward to.

Dumping money into your hobby is investing in your passion. Your passion is tied to your purpose. Never let anyone undermine your hobbies.

Someday the pain will be useful.

Letting people be wrong about you or a situation while keeping your peace and focus is the most misunderstood power move you can make.

We need to change the conversation of what success looks like. It's not to make a billion dollars; it is to wake up in the morning and actually be in a good mood.

You are not lost if no one is looking for you.

Everything is everything, or maybe it's nothing. Either way, it is definitely something.

Your sexiest body part is your mind.

The goal is not money. The goal is the freedom to spend your days how you want.

Love is like a fire. It can warm your heart and burn it to ashes.

Just because you run out of things to post on social media doesn't mean you have to have kids.

Overthinking is a waste of energy. Trust yourself, make a decision, gain experience. There is no such thing as perfect. You cannot think your way into perfection. Just take action.

Never judge yourself too harshly. Be kind to yourself, give yourself time, allow yourself to make mistakes, to be happy and sad.

The best memories come from bad ideas.

If there is even a slight chance of getting something that will make you happy, risk it. Life is too short, and happiness is too rare.

Rabbits jump, and they live for eight years. Dogs run, and they live for 15 years. Turtles do nothing and live for 150 years. Lesson learned.

Creativity is just connecting things. When you ask creative people how they did something, they feel a little guilty sometimes because they didn't do much more than connecting the dots.

Always have a roll of toilet paper in your car.

"Sorry, my cat expects me to be home by now" is a good excuse to leave a party.

The soul usually knows how to heal itself. The challenge is to silence the mind.

Being an adult is mostly just going to bed when you don't want to and waking up when you don't want to.

Cooking is great for your brain. Preparing different dishes requires thinking patterns that train the brain for all kinds of scientific and technical work. And the automatism that encourages us to eat increases the general motivation beyond a serotonin reward.

Your whole life can be thrown off just by associating with someone. Be very selective about who you share your time with.

One day you will meet someone who loves you exactly as you are, and you will gradually discover that they are mentally ill.

If you don't make time for friends, you won't have any.

Always be at the correct end of the dick.

Buy jump-start-cables for your car before you need them.

Never put on a sock before you find the other one.

Insecurity kills more dreams than failure.

Don't stand up in a canoe.

Check the oil in your lawnmower every now and then.

Join animal baby groups on social media. You'll smile more often.

It's not just about removing hurtful or emotionally draining people from your life; it's also about realigning your energy so that you no longer attract these people.

Don't fuck friends, neighbors or co-workers.

Nothing ever goes away until it has taught us what we need to know.

Spend time with people that move you in the direction you want to be going. We absorb the mindset and vibe of the people around us. Being mindful of this helps us share energy with those that naturally help us grow, make healthy choices, and stay inspired.

Decide what you want. Make a fucking plan. And work on that shit. Every. Single. Day.

Be real, not perfect.

Never trust the first price a construction worker gives you.

Squeegee the water from your legs, arms, and torso with your hand before using your towel after a bath or shower.

A mind is like a parachute. It does not work if it isn't open.

Learn to play the piano, at least one or two songs, and don't break promises, even the little ones.

We were all humans until race disconnected us, religion separated us, politics divided us, and wealth classified us.

If you have the power to make someone feel good, you should make them feel good.

Turn off motion blur and chromatic aberration.

After all, we are nothing more or less than what we choose to reveal.

If you must choose between two evils, pick the one you've never tried before.

You can't have too many genuine friends and it's sensible to assess people from time to time. Request something a bit challenging from them. If they're unwilling, you know that your friendship might not be substantial. And, if you feel like you're being taken advantage of, it's time create some space between yourself and those individuals.

If you can't fall asleep, blinking fast for about a minute can help.

Find someone to talk to, even if it's only online. It is important to reflect with somebody outside your own mind. Speaking about your problems helps to guide you towards a solution, even if it's just acceptance. Bottling up can lead to health issues.

Keep your texting to a minimum. Use it primarily to schedule and coordinate dates.

If you search for something specific or rare, and you find it, get it immediately.

Don't go to sleep with an unclear conscience.

The best time to call your ex is at three in the morning while being drunk.

There's always some truth behind 'just kidding', some knowledge behind 'I don't know', some emotions behind 'I don't care', and some pain behind 'it's okay'.

Enjoy yourself; it's later than you think.

Your mood and thoughts are interlinked. Change your thought patterns and break out of negative cycles. Seek help if you feel you cannot do it on your own.

WD-40 contains solvent and can be used for removing things from other things.

Quit your job, buy a ticket, get a tan, fall in love, never return.

Don't adapt to the energy in the room. Influence the energy in the room.

Don't chase. Attract.

Imagination should be used to create reality, not to escape it.

Stop explaining things to people who have already decided not to understand.

Button your shirt from the bottom to the top.

If you figured it all out today, what would be the point of tomorrow? Enjoy the process of being a work in progress.

'Shark-infested waters' is like saying 'human-infested houses'.

Percentages are reversible. 80% of 5 is the same as 5% of 80. Calculate the one that's easier for you.

If it flies, floats, or fucks: rent. You will save a lot of money and hassle.

Sometimes we stress about stress before there's even stress to stress about.

The older you get, the more attractive stability becomes. It's all about peace of mind and a non-stressful environment.

An even remotely rude or disrespectful partner will cause severe problems to your psychological health. Stay away.

You will fall asleep faster if you take a cold shower before bed. Your body prefers a temperature of around 16 - 18 $^{\circ}$C or 61 - 65 $^{\circ}$F for sleeping.

Cooking, cleaning, and doing small repairs around the house and car are basic skills.

Never take out a loan to buy consumer goods like the latest smartphone, a bigger TV, or a fancy car. If you can't pay for it, you can't afford it.

When grocery shopping, always take perishable foods from the back. Food with shorter expiry dates is always placed in the front.

If you want to be happy, you literally must not care what people think. Practice that daily. As long as you are not hurting anybody, do what you want, and be unapologetic about it.

Contrary to popular opinion, quitting is for winners. Knowing when to quit, change direction, leave a toxic situation, demand more from life, give up on something that wasn't working, and move on is a very important skill that people who win at life all seem to have.

Act the way you want to feel. Action kills fear.

Everybody you meet will be either a blessing or a lesson.

Before buying something new, always check if you can get it used. You'll save a lot of money and the planet.

Trust in the timing of your life.

If you have a crush on someone, try to become their friend first. If that doesn't work, move on.

If you need a substance to feel normal, you're an addict.

If your refrigerator stops working, unplug it, defrost it, let it dry, and try to start it again before you call an expensive service.

It's only when you see a mosquito landing on your testicles that you realize that there is always a way to solve problems without using violence.

Check your Bluetooth connection before watching porn.

Every day of your life is practice in becoming the person you want to be.

Always negotiate what you want and how much it will cost when dealing with prostitutes.

Procrastination is like masturbation. It feels good till you realize you've just fucked yourself.

Failure defeats losers but inspires winners.

When someone asks you what you did over the weekend, squint and ask, "Why, what did you hear?"

In the age of distraction, nothing can feel more luxurious than paying attention.

Stretch and drink some water. Think of your posture.

The way to a more productive, more inspired, more joyful life is getting enough sleep.

Don't live your life solely as a wage slave. Build something for your future.

The chances of a piece of bread falling on the carpet jelly side down are directly proportional to the cost of the carpet.

You become a more peaceful person when you stop reacting to people using you as a mirror.

Drugs are not viable long-term power-ups.

One does not have to respond to everyone immediately. Just because we can communicate any time we want, does not mean we have to be available all the time. More often than not, it's nothing personal. People are overwhelmed these days and are just trying to be okay.

It's okay to lose your shit sometimes, because if you keep all your shit, you end up full of shit.

Don't put on lip balm and then kiss your cat.

It's always the ones with the dirty hands pointing fingers.

Social media seriously harms mental health. It is training us to compare our lives, instead of appreciating everything we are. We are in constant fear of missing out. Switch off your phone for a while and enjoy your own life.

Evolve or repeat.

You will always have problems. Learn to enjoy life while solving them.

Wake up early. Exercise. No worries. Fewer screens. More books.

Have a great day pretending everything's normal.

Love your life. Take pictures of everything. Tell people you love them. Talk to random strangers. Do things that you are scared to do. Take your life and make it the best story in the world. Don't waste it.

Make sure you see the candy
before getting in the van.

Your energy is your greatest currency.

Without the freedom to offend, the freedom of expression ceases to exist.

We had empires ran by emperors, we had kingdoms ran by kings, now we have countries...

There are two types of people in this world: those who can extrapolate from incomplete data.

If you are ever tempted to look for outside approval, realize that you have compromised your integrity. If you need a witness, be your own.

You can't fake strong.

Consider everything an experiment.

If a law is unjust, it's not only your right to disobey it; you are obligated to do so.

Some people ride the crazy train. Be sure to drive that motherfucker.

The 97% of the people who quit too soon are employed by the 3% who never gave up.

Pain is inevitable. Suffering is optional.

There are a lot of things you need zero talent for: being on time, making an effort, being high energy, having a positive attitude, being passionate, using good body language, being coachable, doing a little extra, being prepared, and having a strong work ethic.

No requests, no regrets.

Life is not a productivity contest.

Effort is attractive.

Struggling to get your wife's attention? Just sit down and look comfortable.

If you could have it your way, who would you be with, where would you be, and what would you be doing?

Slow progress is still progress.

If you don't mean what you say, shut up.

To learn how to use your head, you have to go out of your mind.

Self-care isn't selfish.

The problem is not the problem. The problem is your attitude about the problem.

Never apologize for burning too brightly.

Keep your hands clean and your mind dirty.

Without a vision for your future, you always return to your past.

This too shall pass. And then some other bullshit will come and take its place.

In the midst of where you are going, don't forget to enjoy where you are.

Some delusion should remain.

An old Cherokee told his grandson, that there is a battle between two wolves going on inside us all. One is Evil. It is anger, jealousy, greed, resentment, inferiority, lies, and ego. The other is Good. It is joy, peace, love, hope, humility, kindness, empathy, and truth. The boy thought about it, and asked "Grandfather, which wolf will win?". And the old man replied, "The one you feed."

Intelligence is the ability to avoid doing work yet getting the work done.

That was then. This is now.

Ordinary people have big TVs. Extraordinary people have big libraries.

Don't we all just really need a day between Saturday and Sunday?

Fascism is cured by reading. Racism is cured by traveling.

May we think of freedom not as the right to do as we please, but as the opportunity to do what is right.

The best revenge is not to be like your enemy.

Depression entices you to get in bed and hide under the covers. It does this over and over until it feels like it's the only safe option. Managing depression means being active and brave. Doing the opposite of safe in order to learn that you can, in fact, handle hard things. By doing so, you create new and healthier ways of thinking.

Sometimes the fear won't go away, so you'll have to do it afraid.

In great attempts, it is glorious even to fail.

Peace sometimes requires you to be quiet even when you're right.

Lack of dedication is an insult to those who believe in you.

Unpleasant truths about ourselves can be the ones we need most. Facing them is vital to our growth.

To plant something is to believe in tomorrow.

Hard work beats talent. Always.

When phones were tied with a wire, humans were free.

Sometimes it's better to just let things be. Let people go. Don't fight for closure, and don't ask for explanations.

When injustice becomes law, resistance becomes duty.

Popularity is for mediocre people.

Don't let a wishbone grow where a backbone should be.

If you believe in karma, you can do bad things to people and assume they deserve it.

Never shake hands sitting down.

Don't enter a pool via the stairs.

If you know how quickly people forget the dead, you will stop living to impress people.

Request the late check-out in a hotel.

Despite what it feels like, sometimes, it's actually not your job to make sure everyone is comfortable, happy, or having fun. Allow people to have their own experiences.

Hold your heroes to a higher standard.

Never be a prisoner of your past. It was just a lesson, not a life sentence.

Always return a borrowed car with a full tank of gas.

Play with passion or don't play at all.

If you need music on the beach, you are missing the point.

People will remember negative experiences over positive experiences.

You not only marry each other, you also marry each other's family and friends. Think about that before you get married.

Life is often really simple, but for some reason, we insist on making it complicated.

Be like a duck. Remain calm on the surface, but paddle like crazy underneath.

Pay attention to your priorities. Do what is most important, not what's most urgent first. Learn to prioritize, and you'll be able to manage whatever life throws at you.

Experience the serenity of traveling alone.

After writing an angry message, read it carefully. Then delete it.

The problem is that intelligent people are full of doubt while stupid people are full of confidence.

Never turn down a breath mint.

Think about what your own eulogy would say if you were to write it today.

The forest was shrinking, but the trees kept voting for the axe, for the axe convinced the trees that, because its handle was made of wood, it was one of them.

So far, you've survived 100% of your worst days.

If tobacco tax is meant to discourage smoking, is income tax meant to discourage working?

Anything that costs you your peace is too expensive.

Nobody wants to get old, but nobody wants to die young either.

If you want to achieve greatness, stop asking for permission.

Give credit. Take the blame.

Never delay kissing or opening a good bottle of wine.

Do what you can, where you are, with what you have.

Stop losing precious days. Stop degenerating into a machine for making money. You are learning nothing in this trivial world of men.

Some of us are just a person who wants to do a lot of things, trapped in the body of a person who wants to sleep a lot.

Common sense is not that common.

Do we have to know who's gay and who's straight? Can't we just love everybody and judge them by the car they drive?

In a century where the media publishes endless stupidities, being cultured is defined not by what you know but what you ignore.

Social media is training us to compare our lives, instead of appreciating everything we are.

No one is going to stand up at your funeral and say "She had a really expensive sofa." or "He had a really nice car." Don't make life about stuff.

Instead of teaching people not to be offensive, we should teach people how not to be offended.

Being afraid to check your bank account is the adult version of being afraid to check your grades.

Never tell your problems to everyone. 80% don't care and the other 20% are glad you have them.

Some people were not put here to evolve.
They are here to remind you what it looks
like if you don't.

The worst part of censorship is ######.

Depression is your avatar telling you it's tired of being the character you're trying to play.

You are overthinking because you really care what happens next. You don't want to fail, and you don't want to let people down. But no amount of planning, worrying, or over-analyzing can give you control over what happens next. Breathe and experience life as it comes.

Inside every old person is a younger person wondering what the fuck happened.

If no one comes from the future to stop you from doing it, then how bad can it be?

Remember, always follow your passion. And if your passion doesn't fit into global capitalism, well, then you are a failure at life.

If you make the biggest smile you can, you will automatically feel happier.

There comes a certain point in your life when sitting at home alone watching TV on a Friday night goes from being super depressing to the most enjoyable part of your week.

No one cares about your efforts, only the results.

No one is going to give you the education you need to overthrow them. Think about that, especially if you have kids.

The people who hid Anne Frank were breaking the law. The people who killed her were following it.

Fabric softener is a waste of money. It can leave a layer of residue on the clothes that may irritate sensitive skin. It will reduce the absorption of towels. Residue can build up in your washing machine, which can lead to mold and mildew problems. And it can also reduce the flame resistance on children's sleepwear.

Never for money. Always for love.

Desperate times call for desperate pleasures.

People will remember not what you said but how you made them feel.

It's easier to get free WiFi than it is to get free water, and people act like nothing is wrong with the world.

Some talk to you in their free time, and some free their time to talk to you. Learn the difference.

Journalism is printing what someone does not want printed. Everything else is public relations.

Money is numbers and numbers never end. If it takes money for you to be happy, your search for happiness will never end.

True happiness is when we are happy with ourselves.

Leave something to the imagination.

One of todays biggest problems is that kids don't dream of building something anymore; they only dream of buying something.

We need more cameras pointed at politicians, not at citizens.

Good judgment comes from experience. And experience comes from poor judgment.

If you've seen one nuclear war, you've seen 'em all.

A dream written down with a date becomes a goal. A goal broken down into steps becomes a plan. And a plan backed by action makes your dreams come true.

To learn who rules over you, simply find out who you are not allowed to criticize.

The person who says it cannot be done should not interrupt the person doing it.

Do it today. Tomorrow it might be forbidden.

Open-minded people embrace being wrong.

Just because you haven't found the right person yet doesn't mean you will.

Inside every cynical person is a disappointed idealist.

Being popular online is like sitting at the cool table in the cafeteria at a mental hospital.

Don't talk, act. Don't say, show. Don't promise, prove.

Dating is a great way to realize that dying alone isn't the worst that could happen.

Normality is a paved road. It's comfortable to walk, but no flowers grow.

It is better to have questions that can't be answered than answers that can't be questioned.

Eat clean. Train dirty.

If you drop your weed on the floor, you can cover a vacuum with a clean sock and get it all back.

If you are not constantly unlearning, dropping bad habits, and adopting new mindsets, you are avoiding the inner work. Remain teachable.

Fast is fine, but accuracy is final. You must learn to be slow in a hurry.

In the end, all you will have learned is how to be strong alone.

Aim to arrive at your death late, in love, and a little drunk.

A mind that is stretched by a new experience can never go back to its old dimensions.

Stop waiting. It's time.

When you are dead, you don't know that you're dead. All of the pain is felt by others. The same thing happens when you are stupid.

Try to remember how you felt before you knew what you know now.

Never argue with stupid people; they will drag you down to their level and then beat you with experience.

Without deviation from the norm, progress is not possible.

Don't be anti-social; be selectively social.

The gender-neutral term for sugar daddy is glucose guardian.

You don't get what you wish for. You get what you work for.

The true sign of intelligence is not knowledge but imagination.

In an avalanche, no single snowflake feels responsible.

The planet doesn't need more successful people. The planet needs more peacemakers, healers, restorers, storytellers, and lovers.

Be careful who you make memories with. Those things can last a lifetime.

A little progress each day adds up to big results.

Your political views should be simple. Be against anything that kills people or destroys the planet we live on.

If you live through defeat, you're not defeated.

Lose yourself to improve yourself.

When the power of love overcomes the love of power, the world will know peace.

Some people are so poor, all they have is money.

People were created to be loved. Things were created to be used. The reason the world is in chaos is because things are being loved and people are being used.

Don't waste your youth with growing up.

Your age is the number of laps you've done around a giant fireball in the center of the solar system.

Work until you no longer have to introduce yourself.

If you don't build your own dreams, someone else will hire you to build theirs.

Train yourself to let go of everything you fear to lose.

A gentleman is simply a patient wolf.

You'll never change your life until you change your habits.

Politicians and diapers must be changed often and for the same reason.

When you're looking for your glasses, always check your head first.

Floppy disks are like Jesus. They died to become the icon of saving.

Jobs fill your pockets, adventures fill your soul.

Before you pray: believe. Before you speak: listen. Before you spend: earn. Before you write: think. Before you quit: try. Before you die: live.

If you are beaten but acquire wisdom, you have won.

Life is a sexually transmitted disease which always ends in death.

Everything happens for a reason; sometimes the reason is you are stupid and make bad decisions.

When was the last time you did something for the first time?

A meal without wine is called breakfast.

We kill people who kill people because killing people is wrong.

Weird is a side effect of awesome.

245

Life is like toilet paper: you're either on a roll or you're taking shit from some asshole.

Until the lion learns how to write, every story will glorify the hunter.

The loneliest people are the kindest, the saddest people smile the brightest, and the most damaged people are the wisest.

Success is like being pregnant. Everyone congratulates, but nobody knows how many times you were fucked.

Know your worth, then add tax.

Hard times create strong people. Strong people create good times. Good times create weak people. Weak people create hard times.

Any society that would give up a little liberty to gain a little security will deserve neither and lose both.

More kissing, less stressing.

Sometimes we go about in pity for ourselves, when all the while a great wind carries us across the sky.

You don't have to be a gynecologist, to know a cunt when you see one.

All palaces are temporary palaces.

Take your pleasures seriously.

Mondays are a symptom of an illness called existence.

Show some fucking passion.

Make yourself a priority.

Offline is the new luxury.

You don't always need a plan. Sometimes you just need to breathe, let go, and see what happens.

Meditate, hydrate, masturbate.

248

You are the artist of your own life. Don't hand the paintbrush to anyone else.

If you love someone, act on it.

Sex is cool, but have you ever fucked the system?

You can never be overdressed or overeducated.

You are personally responsible for becoming more ethical than the society you grew up in.

Always be a little kinder than necessary.

Why explore the universe when we don't know ourselves?

If you wander aimlessly, you will surely fail in your quest.

We are all hoarders and whores.

Happiness is not the absence of problems; it's the ability to deal with them.

It's time to fall back in love with yourself.

What is taken for granted will eventually get taken away.

Smile. You are alive. You've got options.

The things that excite you are not random. They are connected to your purpose. Follow them.

Storms don't last forever.

No reason to stay is a good reason to go.

Earth laughs in flowers.

It's crucial to have an active fantasy life.

Love fast. Kiss slow.

You don't need a reason to help people.

You can't heal if you keep pretending you're not hurt.

The dildo of consequences rarely arrives lubed.

Stop caring about hurting their feelings more than your own.

Your trauma is not your fault. Your healing is your responsibility, though.

There's a difference between people who want to fuck you and people who want to make you cum.

Nothing is absolute. Except that nothing is absolute.

Real is rare.

It's a fine line between being patient and wasting your time.

Stay motivated. Accomplish one thing in the morning, big or small. Use the momentum from it to go on. Realize that life gets better fast. Make a game out of your challenges. Look like a CEO, because you are the CEO of your life. Take a picture of the best part of every day. Recognize and show off your progress.

If some pieces don't fit, it might not be your puzzle.

Your boundary doesn't need an apology.

When you are happy, you enjoy the music. When you are sad, you understand the lyrics.

Don't disconnect from yourself in order to connect with someone.

Don't expect what you don't communicate.

Youth has no age.

Love the skin you are in.

Don't die wondering.

Sometimes you win, sometimes you learn.

Make it simple, but significant.

Be careful who you let on your ship because some people will sink the whole vessel just because they don't like the captain.

Well done is better than well said.

Give homeless people counterfeit money. They'll go to prison eventually and no longer be homeless.

Take a genuine interest in the details of your daily life.

Surround yourself with inspiring beings.

The opinion of ten thousand people is of no value if none of them knows anything about the subject.

Being well-dressed is a form of politeness.

Take care of your three homes: your body, your mind, and your planet.

Doubt even your doubt.

If art is how we decorate space, music is how we decorate time.

The best you ever had is just a memory.

You can disable trucks and cars by puncturing the radiator, fuel tank, or tires with an ice pick or a sharpened screwdriver.

If you are not the lead dog, the scenery never changes.

If you don't make time for your wellness, you will be forced to make time for your illness.

Do whatever you want; just don't hurt people.

You are a spiritual being having a human experience.

If you don't sin, then Jesus died for nothing.

The only dangerous minority is the rich.

Whoever wants music instead of noise, joy instead of pleasure, soul instead of gold, creative work instead of business, passion instead of foolery, finds no home in this trivial world of ours.

Nothing to hide, nothing to say.

It's all fun and foreplay until you want to talk about something other than "How was your day?". Find a partner you can have a conversation with.

Most of us are more concerned with having than with being.

Modern slaves are not in chains; they are in debt.

It's not always a matter of holding the best cards, but sometimes playing a poor hand well.

If the penalty is a fine, then the law only exists for the poor.

Tradition is peer pressure from dead people.

Shine, so that through you, others can see.

Sometimes your silence gives consent.

Normal is an illusion. What is normal for the spider is chaos for the fly.

The temptation of short-term pleasure is the most common prohibitor of long-term success.

It will only affect you if you let it affect you.

The world is changed by your example, not by your opinion.

With money you can buy a house, but not a home. You can buy a doctor, but not health. You can buy a clock, but not time. You can buy a bed, but not sleep. You can buy food, but not an appetite.

True self-care is to build a life that you don't need to escape from.

Take it easy, but take it.

It's a maze without walls.

The only way out is through.

You never know who would love the persona you hide.

Make your mental health a priority.

It's ok to just wander through life, finding interesting things until you die.

Nobody's absence or presence should disturb you inner peace.

Make art, make out, make love.

You'll meet two kinds of people in life: the ones who tear you down and the ones who build you up. In the end, you will thank them both.

Sometimes we create our own heartbreaks through expectations.

Be the energy you want to attract.

Risking is better than regretting.

Successful people never worry about what others are doing.

We've got so many toys and hardly ever play.

Easy doesn't change you.

Stop measuring days by degree of productivity and start experiencing them by degree of presence.

All men are created equal. Then, they get dressed.

What is done in love is done well.

There are two types of 'tired'. One is the need for sleep, one the need for peace.

If you ever break through the ice on a frozen body of water, you have to mitigate your cold shock response by relaxing as much as you can. Try then to get into a horizontal position and push yourself out of the water and onto the ice through swimming motions. Once your upper body is on the ice, crawl away from the hole until it's safe to stand up again.

People who go to war don't want war. People who want war don't go to war.

Live life, forget your age.

Be around those who feed your soul, not eat it.

Let go or be dragged.

Bees don't waste their time explaining to flies that honey is better than shit.

Political correctness is fascism pretending to be manners.

Life is like photography. You need the negatives to develop.

Rise above the storm and you will find sunshine.

Don't count the days. Make the days count.

Stop blaming yourself or others. Learn Feng Shui and blame the furniture.

Empathy without boundaries is self-destruction.

From pain comes knowledge.

Do whatever it takes to make you feel real.

Be the one that makes others want to step up their game.

Loyalty is when they have your back behind your back.

Sex before marriage is considered a sin. Sex after marriage is considered a miracle.

For us, there is only the trying. The rest is not our business.

Be someone who is attached to nothing but attracted to everything.

For artists, there is no such thing as 'time wasted'. Their entire lives are in service to their creative practice.

Being sexy is about being comfortable in yourself.

Thinking is difficult; that's why most people just judge.

Never complain, never explain.

Storms make trees take deeper roots.

Knowledge is knowing that a tomato is classified as a fruit. Wisdom is knowing not to put it into a fruit salad.

The best design trend is to not follow one.

Have more than you show, speak less than you know.

We are our choices.

People who don't know how to relax hate people who know how to relax.

Just because someone carries it well, doesn't mean it isn't heavy.

Life and beer: chill for best results.

Old keys won't open new doors.

Be brave enough to suck at something new.

Sometimes life puts us in the same situation again to see if we're still dumb.

Suffer the pain of discipline or suffer the pain of regret.

If it doesn't matter, get rid of it.

The body achieves what the mind believes.

Find the kind of partner you don't have to clean your browser history for.

A man is lucky if he is the first love of a woman. A woman is lucky if she is the last love of a man.

No matter how straight you are, your hand is bisexual.

Leave your washing machine door open after using it to let it dry out and prevent mold from growing inside.

A 'butt' was a medieval unit of measure for wine. Technically, a buttload of wine is about 475 liters or 126 gallons.

Nothing you buy will transform the hole into a whole.

True terror is to wake up one day and discover that your high school class is running the country.

Slow success builds character; fast success builds ego.

One big difference between men and women is that if a woman says 'smell this', it usually smells nice.

In the evening there is feeling.

In the morning there is meaning.

Lovesickness is a luxury.

People are like whiskey. Some go down better than others.

Leave the world a better place than you found it.

Doubting yourself is normal. Letting it stop you is a choice.

Fill your own cup and let them fall in love with the overflow.

You're only competing with yourself. If you believe otherwise, you're doing it wrong.

Faith is not a virtue; it is the glorification of voluntary ignorance.

The more we value things outside our control, the less control we have.

Never before has a generation so diligently recorded themselves accomplishing so little.

Have the courage to be disliked.

Love is like a fart. If you have to force it, it's probably shit.

Fill your brain in the afternoons with books, learning, and socialization. Empty your brain before bed with journaling, planning, and meditation. Use your brain in the morning with creation, output, and focus.

Keep every stone they throw at you. You've got castles to build.

Anything you are desperate for will run from you.

The secret of getting ahead is getting started.

Learn to be indifferent to what makes no difference.

You can fill a water bottle with a little bit of water and put it in the freezer. Once it is frozen, you can top it up with water to have ice-cold water to go.

The timing of your life will make sense one day.

Obstacles don't block the path. They are the path.

All we have is now.

Some of the best moments in life are the ones you can't tell anyone about.

Pleasure is the whole point. We are made for pleasure. Humans have not survived out of spite or sheer grit. We live for pleasure. We're made to fill our bellies with delicious food, take naps in soft grass, to touch each other in joy and comfort.

Being surrounded by the wrong people can be the loneliest thing in the world.

The absence of knowledge often produces the presence of fear.

Life needs more slow dances in the kitchen.

Poverty exists not because we cannot feed the poor, but because we cannot satisfy the rich.

Don't try to create and analyze at the same time. They are different processes.

The point of propaganda is not only to misinform or push an agenda. It is to exhaust critical thinking and to annihilate the truth.

A ship in harbor is safe, but that is not what ships are built for.

Never back down, never give up.

Bullets only do their jobs after they're fired.

A new study shows you can get people to believe anything as long as you say 'a new study shows' before whatever you say.

It's life. You are not going to figure it out. You just climb up on the beast and ride.

A private life is a happy life. People cannot ruin what they don't know.

Whenever you are upset, just imagine a T-Rex making a bed.

If you don't drink, how will your friends know you love them at two in the morning?

Better done than perfect.

Reading a book is pretty surreal. You stare at markings on slices of dead trees and hallucinate vividly.

A happy ending depends on where you end your story.

NOTES

THANK YOU SO MUCH THAT YOU SPENT TIME AND/OR
MONEY ON THIS BOOK. I LOVE YOU.

HERE ARE SOME TIPS ON
HOW TO SUPPORT AUTHORS
WITHOUT SPENDING MONEY:

- Connect, like, subscribe
- Review the book on Amazon
- Post about the book on social media
- Tell a friend, or 20, about the book
- Ask you local library to add the book to their collection

CHECK OUT

www.giantblur.com

FOR MORE